the cool side of the pillow

Charles Lytton

Book design by PenworthyLLC
Original line art by Patsy Faires
Other graphics reproduced
with permission of clipart.com/Getty Images

ISBN: 09852732-0-8 EAN-13: 978-0-9852732-0-0

This book is dedicated to the five most interesting people in the world! Each and every time I see them I am amazed by how big they are, how worldly they have become and just how much they know. I dedicate The Cool Side of the Pillow *to my five grand-daughters: Tyler Anderson, Lilly Anderson, Charlie Schoenig, Avery Anderson and Brooke Anderson. They add new meaning to the phrase "You sure can learn a lot from* The Cat in the Hat.*"*

CONTENTS

THE COOL SIDE OF THE PILLOW   iii to v

A BOY IN THE COUNTRY

Walking Barefooted   3

Some of the Stuff I've Eaten   6

Goose Paté Cognac   10

The First Television I Ever Saw   13

The Things That I Have Pissed On   16

Kate   19

Now I Was a Climber   23

SPEED BLEEDING

Garland Little and Me Sleigh Riding   29

Bicycles and Bicycles   33

Other Things with Wheels 51

DOWN THE RIVER

The Creek 57

My Day Finally Came 64

The Old Paddle 66

The Bus 69

The Crosstie Cabin 74

Me and Old Ted 81

A Watchdog that Did Not Need to Bark 82

The Time I Rode a Log Downriver to Fishing Run 85

Life's Little Lessons 88

A Reputation Follows You 91

Paddling the Canoe Through the Cabin Door 94

My First Canoe 98

White Water, White Knuckles 105

Rock Diving 111

The Big Tree in the River 118

Oh, Just to Sit on the Whiterock 121

The Day I Left the River 124

TRAPPING...GIGGING...SKINNING CRITTERS

Putting Myself Through Junior High School   131

Squirrel Hunting While at School   134

Sprayed by a Dead Skunk   138

Sucker Gigging   142

The Big Turtle   148

The Fine Art of Trotline Fishing   151

The Best Fish I Ever Saw   155

Muskrat Trapping in the New River   161

The Sweet Smell of Wood Smoke and Perfume   168

You Can Learn a Lot from a Groundhog   176

TO SOME THEY ARE JUST MEMORIES   183

THE COOL SIDE
OF THE PILLOW

I grew up in a little four-room cinderblock house on River Ridge (which is in the southwest part of Virginia, right along the New River). We did not have a bathroom, just a two-hole outhouse. The house was just a rock's throw from my grandmother's and Uncle Shorty's houses. It was two throws to Uncle Nelson's house.

I said rock's throw because on River Ridge we had lots of rock, yellow and orange flint, to be more accurate. I must have picked up around a million or more of them and pitched them over the hill, only to have discovered that during the night two other rocks had come back in their place. You know, in all of my rock picking-up and pitching, I never once tossed a stone or even saw one. I guess only town boys see and was taught to throw stones.

In the summer it would be so hot at night that if you strained a little you could hear lizards lying out in the dark trying to catch their breath. Elmer – that's my dad -- said, "If you work hard enough during the day, you will go right to sleep like you were on the North Pole."

If I complained a little he would find me another garden to hoe, some locust trees to skin, or some brush that needed to be cut. In the summer my family kept me plenty busy without any extra jobs. But, there were nights when the sheets got wet from my head to my toes. These were not the normal wet dreams experienced by young men. I would lie awake and sweat, but I sure never said a word to anyone. I knew that their treatment for complaints would be to work a few more rows in the garden. They might have made me stop using the motorized lawn mower and go back to the push-type reel mower. Oh goodness, I wanted that old mower to stay under the smokehouse. Who knows? They might even have come up with another new way to encourage relaxation. I had heard rumors about (again) picking up buckets of small rocks in the garden and carrying them to the mud holes in Grandmother's driveway. That had come close to just killing me the last time I did it. I would just lie there thinking of fans, lying buck naked in a snowdrift and something that I had read about called an "air conditioner." (Note that I could and did read!)

Sooner or later when the clock got on around to 1:00 or 2:00 a.m., a light cool breeze would come through the window and I would drift off to sleep. Man, how I loved those cool August breezes. In some ways it was worth all of the sweating just for the great feelings the cool breezes brought with them. You want to talk about something good? In August, the late evening summer rains came -- Grandmother always called them "sweet summer rains" -- and made the corn fill out and stuff grow. They made for good sleeping, too.

Now, there were times when the late night cool breezes

did not come. There were times when it would not rain, no matter how much you prayed. You could just look out the window and see the lightning miles away. "Well, someone else is sleeping," I would say to myself, "but it ain't me."

Another treatment for the heat was to sleep on the floor. Many summer nights I would pull my pillow off the bed and sleep on the cool wood floor. My sweaty back would stick to it and make funny sounds, like I had flatulence, when I rolled over. It was real hard, and believe it or not sometimes in the night when the sweat dried up on me, I got to feeling too cold. I would jump back in the bed, just a-shivering to boost my body temperature. Sleeping in the summertime in that little cinder-block house was hard work.

But, I did find a magnificent cure for summertime heat. One night, before the evening breezes came to my window, I rolled over. For some reason I turned my pillow over and gave it a good fluffing. When I lay back down, my head rested on the most wonderful thing that was -- "The Cool Side of the Pillow." In this life, I have taken for granted some of the best things there are, such as a cold glass of buttermilk, summer rain, a walk in autumn woods, the taste of fresh snow flavored with Kool Aid, a shaded porch swing and the smell of fresh-mown hay. I even like the feeling of sweat running down my back when I have earned it. But, I have never taken for granted the feeling of the "Cool Side of the Pillow." It just makes me sleepy to think about it.

A BOY

IN THE COUNTRY

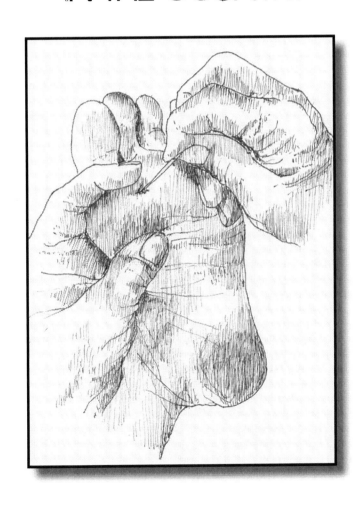

Walking Barefooted

Going barefooted is one of the things that separate town people from country people. Town boys go shopping for shoes, while country boys go shopping for fishhooks and shotgun shells. Town boys look through the windows of the store for new clothes, while country boys sit in the woods wishing for a new shotgun and fishing rod. Sit and talk to any good old boy long enough, and there will come a time when he (sometimes she) will lean back in the chair, on the two back legs, and start talking about that first walk barefooted in the spring. How your feet are as tender as a baby's butt after a winter of being bound up in shoes. They will tell you stories about liking to stand in the melted tar on the road in the summer and feel the tar squish up between their toes. Some will even talk about stumping their toe on a big rock on the way back from fetching the milk cows. I can even tell you about the time I stepped right into a fresh pile of cow shit. Daddy said, "That will teach you to watch out where you are going. Now, go to the pond and wash that stuff off of your feet." Notice no mention was made of going home to wash.

If I had time, I would tell about the day I stepped on a big blackberry briar coming back from the river. After a while your feet looked like -- and were as tough as -- the horse harness resting on eighty-penny nails on the side of the barn. It takes a lot of time for your mother to dig through the callus to get the briars out or let it fester until the briar wanted to come out on its own. I always thought that being shot in the foot could not have hurt much more than Momma digging out a deep briar. You might limp for a while after such hurtful treatment, but the thorns had to come out. I guess it does sound like there are some negative points that come with going barefooted, and there are, but they are all worth it when you think about that first walk of the spring in the cool morning dew.

One of the best parts of being a true Appalachian American boy and pure-blooded River Ridge specimen is measured by how early you can officially go barefooted. The real joy is not in walking in a late snow, but just saying you did it. The great feeling is not simply being man -- or boy -- enough to make a nighttime run to the Johnny house with a frost on the ground. It is just that you made the run barefooted!

You can bet that first walk of the season in the morning dew is going to be cool. The hard calluses on your feet even soften up and welcome the experience. Your whole body takes on a cool feeling. It is so refreshing that even the honeybees tend to get out of your way and choose to wait and sting some other day.

Have you ever seen a spider's web made by one of them real big yellow garden spiders? The dew holds to the web way up into the morning just to show off nature's beauty. Sometimes a staub gets ground into your foot so deep that only limping along the shallow ledge near the bus fishing can soften up the calluses enough to let your mama start to dig it out.

To the true connoisseur of barefootedness, there is a big difference between walking in dew and walking in wet grass after a rain. There's also a big feeling difference between dew-wet grass and grass wet by fog. Rain-wet grass allows your feet to go all the way to the soil. Fog-wet grass is very soothing in its own right, but it deprives the body of the visual experience that fresh morning dew gives.

I do not want to get too poetic here, but you can see the flowers better and appreciate their smell with the early morning dew on them! There isn't anything like it.

Some of the Stuff
I Have Eaten

We did eat like kings some of the time. Jimmy Bland seemed to have a limitless supply of Beanie Weenies that were real good. Still are, when I eat them once in a while, just to remember the canoe trips, hunting expeditions and bad flatulence. As good as they are, though, my mainstays were sardines and Vienna sausage. I remember when Jimmy Bland showed up with two cans of sardines packaged in hot sauce. I thought, "What can they think up next?"

I loved the cans of breakfast sausage, too. You just put it in the pan and heated it all the way through and mounted it on fried bread. You had a meal fit for a king. Why, you did not even need eggs or sweet milk to make that good.

Each year in the very early fall, my family would kill two or three hogs. They were the small ones, weighing no more than 250 pounds. Today that is a good-size hog, but back then

6

you tried to raise them big. Well, anyway, every time we went to the bus down by the river, I would take a one-pound pack of sausage with me for breakfast. We made whole hog sausage, which means everything went into it except the tenderloin.

Now, for us, sausage grease had a lot of uses. You could always fry eggs in the grease. To do this correctly you needed at least one and a half inches of boiling grease. More grease is always better. You want the eggs to stay in about their original shape while they cook. If you use lots of grease, the eggs won't flatten out much, you see. Also, they won't stick.

The grease could be turned into gravy, really good gravy, I might add. Back then I did not make that much gravy, because mine always turned out lumpy. Every red-necked boy knows it's just a plain fact that you cannot eat lumpy gravy as good as you can regular, smooth gravy. Lumpy gravy has the capacity to glob you up in your insides or something; it might cause awful things to go wrong. Chuck was a good gravy maker; his just never got lumpy. Not even his specialty trout gravy. Why, I have seen him take the pan off the stove, set it on the floor of the log cabin over on the creek, stir in flour real careful-like, and then set it back on the stove to lightly brown the flour and add in milk or water. Never a lump. Good gravy is kind of like a religious experience for a boy growing up on River Ridge.

One evening Chuck had fried up a large pan of fresh-caught trout. They were real crispy and brown. He had also made about one gallon of fresh-trout gravy. Everyone wanted a fish and some gravy. Well, everyone but one. This one fellow said that he wanted one so bad -- being brown and crispy with the gravy smelling so good -- but he questioned the sanitation in the cabin. We all tried to put his mind at ease; there was no sanitation, none at all. Just eat and enjoy!

Another time we were gigging just after Thanksgiving. Everybody killed hogs at Thanksgiving. Someone, I think it was Eph Page, showed up. We had had a big cooking fire going for a while. Eph said that he had fresh pig's feet to cook. Everyone else said, "Good! Bring them out." I was sent to the weeds to get the sliding board. Pappy had an old children's playground sliding board that we laid right in the fire as our cooktop. The old pans were quickly cleaned, so the pig's feet could be put in them to boil a little. Then a great big dollop of last year's lard was set to melting in the big cast-iron skillet.

Eph chopped each pig foot right down the middle with an ax. Each half was rolled in flour and very carefully placed in the grease. If you dropped one you could set the world on fire or burn one of your hands off up to the elbow or both. The hog's feet cooked a minute or two on each side until they got right brown. They were set on the bucket lid. We had a rule when we were gigging against extra dishes. Most of the time you just got the hot stuff out of the pan and somehow held onto it withe your pocketknife until you worked up the nerve to stick it in your mouth.

For me, hog's feet always fell into a category all their own. I had to work up the nerve to start on mine. Early comers to the gigging got one. Mine was right tough, and as usual after you fought your way through the skin and leftover hair, there was no meat to speak of. Everyone seemed to just love them, though. Thinking back, I guess I did, too. I guess anything cooked over an open fire in the cool night air is good. Throw in an air-cooled Blue Ribbon or two. Just never you mind the grit, dirt, burnt tough bone, gristle, fat, salt and wood ashes.

Pig's feet were a kind of food that you did not tell people you ate. They were considered a by-product from hog killing, in the same classification as chitterlings. Eating pig's feet will do nothing for your social standing in the community.

Goose Paté Cognac

I will bet that it is spelled wrong, and I have no clue how to spell it or even how to say it. I think that it is French, and if it ain't, it ort to be. Well, let me explain.

Chuck, Jimmy, and Mr. Shorter are at the bus, for sure, possibly The Woolf and Growler, too, are setting around there one morning. I am there, also. It is one of those early fall days that just seem to stick in my mind. Most likely it is the most perfect day ever. I can judge fine days by this memory. There is just the faintest trace of early fall color in the trees. You have got to look close, but it is there. Also, the many colors of green are reflected back in the river. There is the slightest breeze in the air, but not one riffle on the water. The river has a clean and pleasant smell, kind of like the Old New River just wants someone to come and go swimming. The night has been cool, and the sun is working hard to push the air temperature toward 80°. There are no boats on the river and no trains going by making any noise. The Radford Arsenal is even quiet. Only a few distant birds are calling, and occasionally one may fly by. The river is as flat as a pancake with a clear reflection of the sky and early reds and yellows of the trees. The only disturbance to the calm water is an occasional fish jumping. The water is so quiet that any riffle from his jump would reach both shores. Days like this one are what River Ridge Boys live for, and they just never forget!

This was the morning that Mr. Shorter said, "Isn't the river placid?" I looked to see what he was talking about in the river; I could not find the plastic or anything he was talking about. I looked again. Jimmy and Chuck looked, too. They may tell you that they did not look, but out of the corner of my eye I saw their movement. Mr. Shorter said, "Jimmy, I did not think that these two knotheads would know what I was talking about, but I am disappointed in you. Placid means quiet and peaceful."

Mr. Shorter had been visiting his family in Callins, Virginia, down near Danville. They had had a fancy party of some kind. Joe had brought us the leftovers. While he liked a good joke as much as the next person, he was not given too much to outward laughter, but he was different this day. There must have been 10 little cans of potted meat or some kind of potted ham and some unsalted flat little crackers that he passed out. We started tasting the stuff, and Joe would kind of roll his eyes and chuckle watching us. To me it tasted right strong and greasy, in a slick kind of way. I just could not put my finger on it.

Now, I am just speaking for myself here, but I would have been hard-pressed to have eaten more than five or six cans, if Mr. Shorter hadn't been there. I did not like the stuff. I had done made up my mind about this. Hell, I could not even read the label; it was written in some language other than American. I wasn't eating no whole lot of it. Mr. Shorter said it was a good kind of goose liver paté in cognac sauce. I was right -- it was no potted ham. I will always think that placid rivers and paté go together. I think that Joe was right. Even today when things are going real good, I sometimes say, "That is right placid, ain't it?" Notice that I did not add in any paté; you can just keep that stuff.

I just loved to be around Chuck Shorter's family. Uncle Walter and Aunt Evelyn lived in Lynchburg, Virginia. When we would visit, they would always send out for a very large bucket of Kentucky Fried Chicken and a box of Blue Ribbon Beer. Chuck had told her that I had taken an art class in high school, so she took the time to show me her art collection. The collection included a real Picasso. While I was looking at the pencil drawing of this fellow, I set my beer can down on the table. Aunt Evelyn screamed like a wild cat! I grabbed the can and ran for the door. It turns out this table came from the home of some very famous Englishman. Someone like Queen Guinevere or Mary Queen of Scots or such. "Nothing but the best polish and cotton cloth has touched this table in more than century." That goose paté in cognac may have tasted bad, but it had done nothing for my refinement or culture. When Aunt Evelyn squalled at me, I jumped three feet.

The First Television
I Ever Saw

A few months back we bought one of those large flat-screen televisions. It is no more than three inches thick and has at least a 24-inch screen. The people look almost life-size, and the picture is as clear as spring water. I am watching the modern marvel when — you guessed it—my fat little mind starts to wonder off to a much earlier time. Have you noticed your brain often does that? I think that I must have a touch of attention-wondering-off-syndrome, or AWOS.

I am going to try to be real honest here with you. Some of this story I do remember, but some of it I just think I can remember. Once in while growing up I heard things, and now I sometimes cannot tell what is truly one of my memories and what is a tale from listening to others talk. Well, anyway, after I had written this story, I took a copy over to Mother. After she and I read it, she added a little more, so now I do think it is real accurate.

In or about 1956, we got our very first television. It was at least as tall as me and much wider. Truly it was at least three feet tall and at least three feet deep. There was no place in our house for such a behemoth of a thing. Daddy made a wooden platform over the downstairs banisters. The TV backed up to the east window of the house. When you turned it on, you got lots of static and many little lines going up and down. Sitting right on top, it had a big set of rabbit ears. As for the TV shows. I can only remember "Howdy Doody," and that is about it. Mother said there were two or three others.

The local people are what I do remember most. People came each night to watch TV. There was Mr. Luther and Miss Mamie, Shorty and Mamaw, Toot and Uncle Nelson, Mod and Ethel. Also, there was a limitless supply of Kool-Aid, popcorn and coffee.

Daddy was working the four until midnight shift at the Radford Arsenal, so he missed almost all of the fun. Momma had to get ready for the evening's entertainment. "In the beginning it was exciting having the whole community come to the house. I liked it, and the community did, too," said Momma Ruth. After a few weeks, all the sugar had done been licked off the candy sucker, so to speak. She was turning into a short order cook, and it was getting expensive.

Each night that the TV was on, there were great big messes left on the floor to clean up. There was spilt beer, walked-on popcorn, sticky Kool-Aid spills and more. Each night, Momma cleaned up the mess before Elmer made it home. Then Elmer's work shift changed, and he made it home for Television Night. He was shocked! Kids and visitors came from everywhere. The mess covered the small living room floor, and Momma was just running up and down the stairs to the kitchen taking short orders like in a restaurant. Well, Old Elmer just kind of came unglued. He sent everyone home and helped clean up the mess. He got mad at the community and took the TV out and vowed never to have another one until someone else got a TV.

Sometime later we got a second TV. With the new TV came the "Ozzie and Harriet Show." Before I knew it, "I Love Lucy" had come on, too. When I was about 13 or 14, I went to Mason Williams' barbershop and found out that TV-watching would never be the same. He had traded his old black and white set for one that would play in color. Like those people a few years earlier at my house, I now went to the barbershop each night. I saw "Bonanza" in color for the first time up at Mason's. I had to get there early if I wanted a chair. If I was late, I would have to stand or set in the floor. Little Joe, Hoss, Ben and Adam, now they had it made!

The Things That I Have Pissed On

Some people tell me that bragging about bodily functions, like peeing or farting, for example, is a country boy thing. I don't know about such things as that, but true red-blooded River Ridge Appalachian boys did experiment with this phenomenon. I must admit right here and now that I, too, have done a little experimenting with peeing. Yes, I found it to be a lot of fun!

One of my first pleasurable experiences came when I was about 10 years old. There was a big chestnut oak that stood right behind my homeplace, down over the hill from our hog lot, leaning over a cliff toward the New River. The old tree was at least 60 feet tall, and the cliff it stood on was 125 feet high with the Norfolk and Western Railroad at its foot. At one time, I just loved to crawl out and set on the big limbs. I could feel the breeze, watch people fishing on the river, and count railroad cars as the trains passed under me. I just enjoyed the freedom; it was almost like flying. As a 10-year-old, I never once even thought about falling to my death on the railroad tracks below.

I think I climbed this tree for two reasons, and peeing on trains would be the third reason. My first reason was for the fun of it. The second was to hear my mother and grandmother come to the top of the hill and scream down over the bluff at me: "Now get your butt (they said something else, but butt will work just fine right here) out of that damn tree before you fall down on the railroad. If you fall out, you'd better hope that the train cuts you into little pieces. If it doesn't, you are going to be in real trouble." I just lived to hear them holler at me. I knew that neither one of them was going to come over that steep hill after me.

In the beginning, I never even thought about the thrill of peeing on a train. Then one day, there I sat, and the train was bearing down on me. I said to myself, "I just wonder if I could pee right on top of that locomotive, just behind the thing that touches the electrical wires." Yes, you read that correctly.

In the early days, electrical trains were the norm. Diesels did not come around until I was older. The trains behind the house ran on electricity. There were two great big non-insulated wires almost over the center of the railroad tracks, and a train engine had a carriage mounted on the top that stayed in constant contact with those wires. This was how the locomotive received power to run the gigantic electric motors.

It took a lot of good aiming and a lot of body power, but I

did it. To pee on the locomotive in proper fashion, I had to pee between the wires just behind the carriage, or I would miss the locomotive altogether. According to my rules of train-peeing that was a no-no. You see, I knew the Peeing Rules by heart, because I made them up. So, I just had to practice peeing every time I climbed the tree.

Everyone thought that I was just tree-climbing, until one very pretty fall afternoon when Uncle Shorty just quietly asked me, "What did you just do?" Shorty had been setting over the bluff squirrel-hunting, and I did not see him. Well, I bragged on my train-peeing. He said that I was just plain lucky and that was all there was to it. "One of these days you are going to pee right on those wires just right, and an electrical charge is going to burn your peter right off all the way back to the far side of your butt. Now get out of that tree," he demanded. I did, and never peed on any other trains when anybody was looking, especially electric trains.

KATE

Kate, yes Kate, I do have good memories of Kate. There was Kate Guynn, Old Miss Kate, Katherine Kate Evans — all three were fine, female human Kates. But they are not the Kate in this story.

This Kate was one of the most gentle females I have ever known. She was good-natured in all weather. She had those big round brown eyes that never blinked. She seemed to look right through me. She had right coarse, straight brown hair, too. Did I tell you that she was a mule? Well, she was.

I bet Old Kate did not weigh more than 600 pounds and was probably more than 25 years old. Chuck Shorter owned her. Up until this point her life had been spent coming to the hay truck in the morning. She grazed away in the shade of the willows along the creek. Occasionally, she would be seen swishing her tail to knock off a few flies. That was about it. Where Chuck found Old Kate I do not know. She was just one of the many animals in the menagerie he kept on the farm.

Chuck said that she knew how to work. But, I had never seen her do anything except eat. I just feel compelled to tell you that mules are smart. Often they are smarter than the humans that claim to own them or work with them.

Chuck Shorter was in a fence-building mood. For the previous few days, he had been cutting fence posts over across the creek up in a very steep hollow. He had cut down many locust trees. To do this, he had walked through some of the thickest and most fierce blackberry briars in the county. These were old briars with thousands of dead canes covered with thorns the size of hummingbird beaks and sharp as razors. Some of them briars had been dead since long before I was born. If I got one in me, it would not turn loose until my mother hooked a very large needle in it and pulled real hard. Often it felt like she just pushed the briar on through to the other side of my leg.

The morning came when it was time to cut the limbs off the trees and drag them tree trunks down into the holler where they could be sawed into fenceposts. The simple way to get the posts out of the holler would have been to drag them out with Chuck's "C" Farmall Tractor. But, unfortunately the holler was too steep to safely use the tractor. So an alternative method had to be used. Yes, you got it. Old Kate came to the rescue!

I know; I was there. My brother Melvin, "The Woolf," and Chuck were in attendance as well. Jimmy Bland might have been there, too. Most likely there were others, but 40 or 50 years have robbed me of that recollection. Chuck caught Old Kate and put a makeshift harness on her back. The old girl just stood there. I walked her across the creek; she stopped. and took a long drink. Then she just started walking up the hill and into the hot, briar-ridden, steep hollow. It was like she knew exactly what to do and what was coming next.

When we got back in the hollow, I walked her up beside the first log, and Woolf attached one end of the chain around the butt end of a log. The other end of the chain he hooked on the single-tree on Old Kate's harness. I made a clucking sound a time or two, and she just stood there. So I clucked at her a few more times and flipped the drive-lines across her back. She just stood there. So I clucked a few more times, rapped her with lines and hollered, "GET UP, KATE" as loud as I could.

Old Kate took off. I do not want you to think that she just started off. No, no, she started running fast. She went from standing still to a fast canter, and then a high lope in one step. The log behind her was only hitting the high places on the ground. I could not keep up with her, and I fell down. I was still holding the drive-lines and could not turn them loose. I was screaming, "Whoa, whoa, stop!" The more I screamed, the faster she went. The louder I screamed, the quicker her steps.

She was running at a full gallop with me and the log. She dragged me over fresh-cut stumps. I went through fresh-cut locust brush piles. Then she turned and headed for a briar patch. She did not miss one brush pile, either. I was truly afraid to turn loose of the lines, because the log might have run right over me. All of a sudden, she just stopped. She was standing beside Chuck. The sorry rascal could not unhook the log chain, because he was laughing so hard. To Chuck and Woolf, it is funny that I had just grubbed the hillside clean with my chest. I had been working real hard to grow them hairs on my chest, and now both of them had been dragged off.

Well, somehow we made it through the day. The post got drug out. Old Kate proved her worth, and she went back to grazing. I set to digging the blackberry thorns out of my body, and concentrated real hard on re-growing lots of skin and them two chest hairs. All the while, I was nursing my sore ribs and chest. Yes, Old Kate could work, and I am just the man who can show you the scars to prove it. Chuck and Woolf cannot tell you anything at all. I do not think that they even saw much. All they did was roll around and laugh.

Now I Was a Climber

Climbing trees is just part of being a red-neck boy. Everybody I knew climbed trees. We did it for the fun of it and to hone our skills when the time came for showing off. I think that I learned my tree-climbing in the big white oak in the backyard. Grandmother could sit on the porch and holler, "You are going to fall out and get yourself killed or something worse." The more she hollered the higher I went. I never gave one thought to falling out. I just loved the feeling of air as the tree moved in the wind. When a limb broke one time, I came crashing down and landed in the coal pile, but I did not get one scratch.

Once, I had a small four-board treehouse right up in the top of that tree, out on little tiny limbs. I could crawl out there and watch the world go by. One windy night, the treehouse was blown clean out of the tree. All that Elmer ever said was, "I am glad that those boards did not hit the car."

Out in Mr. Luther's field there were three or four very

large old cherry trees. In the early summer, when cherries were ripe, I would spend many hours racing the birds for my share of the fruit. I would eat no less than a gallon each day until they were gone. I never fooled around with the low branches. I went right to the top and picked the little branches clean. I liked the cherries up where the wind and sun had had their way with them; I thought they were sweeter. I just know that this is right; for those are the ones the birds eat first. I know that this made the birds mad when they saw me coming, because those are also the ones they liked. Once in a while, Mom would call out to me to come and get a bucket and pick enough for a pie. Again, never once did they caution me about falling out or breaking my arm, or head for that matter. But, I did hear her say, "Now be real careful and don't break the limbs. That might make Mr. Luther mad." Today most of the cherry stumps are long since rotted away.

At one time there was a massive old hemlock over in the spring hollow. It was down over the hill from Gilbert Hilton's house. This was a great tree to climb. The first limbs started about six or eight feet from the ground. I would go right to the top, high enough to be almost even with Mod Snider's driveway. There was a great view of the river and trains coming up from Whitethorn. If Gilbert or Mod saw me, they would call down over the hill and tell me to get out of that tree before I fell. I was just too hard-headed to listen, and I knew (and they did too) that Mom and Dad were not coming to check on me. It was just too far for either of them to walk down over the hill. Besides, I was 10 or 11 years old and had done been turned out. I kind of came and went as I wished. Today, the tree is gone, so is the old spring, and the hollow even looks smaller.

The one thing that I climbed that I wish I had not was a telephone pole at Prices Fork Elementary School. I was in the second grade, but dumb enough to still be in kindergarten. One morning before school, some of the big kids were taking turns climbing the telephone pole with a basketball goal nailed on it. They were good. They just wrapped their legs around the pole, inched their way up, got aholt of the basketball rim, swung out and dropped. It sure looked like fun. I was a good climber, too, but I needed limbs and lots of them, because I was right round through my middle. It was not long before the big kids lost interest in climbing the telephone pole and moved on to play baseball. I took up mastering that telephone pole. I wrapped my fat little legs around the pole and squeezed it hard, held on with my arms and inched my legs up. I was making some headway, but not much.

I was up maybe five feet or less from the ground when the morning bell for school rang. Now I was in a tough predicament. I had never thought about how to get down, so I just kind of turned loose and slid down the pole. I ran a splinter deep into my right thigh. It stung like fire. I knew that if I told Miss White, my teacher, she would want to dig the splinter out. That is not what bothered me. I did not have on underwear and did not want anyone to know this. Plus, I did not want her to see me naked. I just knew she would tell everyone about the no-underwear thing. So, I just sat there all day, and the fire in the creosote splinter grew by the hour.

Finally, the school day ended. When I sat down on the bus my whole leg was hurting. Once the bus dropped me at home and I was firmly on my own ground, right there in the edge of the driveway in the shade of the red oak, I dropped my britches to the ground. I took to squeezing and pulling at that splinter until it turned loose. By damn, I pulled it out! I was unaware that everyone on the bus was watching me and laughing. I did not see or hear all the men in cars stopped behind the bus. There I was buck-naked from the waist down. I still did not have underwear on.

I had the splinter out. I would worry about the kids' laughter tomorrow. When I showed Daddy my big splinter and the big red spot on my leg, he said, "It would have hurt a lot more if it had stuck in something else." No sympathy, just a big scrubbing with lye soap and lots of iodine and a dose of Black Draught and a thick gob of Raleigh Salve. The iodine was for the infection, and the laxative for prevention of future illness or something. The salve was to make it heal up. I did wear my pair of white underwear the next day just in case I had to show off my wound and splinter.

SPEED BLEEDING

Garland Little and Me Sleigh Riding

When I grew up on River Ridge, we would not miss school for snow in the winter unless there was a good six or seven inches. This story starts off in one of those colder snowy times.

I am at least 16 years old. Mom and Dad's personal car is a VW bus. The road is solid packed-down snow and ice. It is very slick, and I need to go to the store.

(Here is just a little aside. If I was the Daddy and you were the 16-year-old driver, I would say to you, "If you are going to the store tonight walk. You are not driving the VW bus down that slick hill." Neither Ruth nor Elmer says this to me, so I drive the VW bus to Long Shop.)

I set around the store with Dirty Neck Wiley for a while, and not one person comes out other than me. I am just about to head for home, when in walks Garland Little. He lives only about 200 feet away from the store.

We set around the store enjoying the cheese, a Pepsi Cola and a retelling of some of the better stories. The subject of sleigh-riding comes up. Dirty Neck tells about how when he was boy, they would hook their sleds together and someone would drag all of the sleds to the top of the Bob Price Hill. Then they would race back.

I ask, "What if two sleds wanted to cross the creek bridge at one time?"

"There was no bridge back then," says Dirty Neck. "You just raced across the frozen creek."

I ask, "What if you could not slow down in time? Would you hit the big White Oak Tree at the ESSO Station"?

"Weren't no gas station then either. The only gas around here was out front of this store," Dirty Neck goes on to explain. "The only thing you had to worry about was a horse or a cow being out or the big White Oak Tree in the turn of the road."

After a while, I say that I am headed for home, and Garland asks me to pull his sled to the top of the Sucker Snider hill. I have no sled, so this is going to be a ride for Garland Little, not me. I go to get a hay string from out of John Blackburn's barn, tie his sled onto the back of the VW bus and start up the hill, going straight with no trouble and never slipping one time. When we stop just behind Sam Smith's house, Garland says something like, "I bet this sled will go 30 miles per hour down this hill."

Like a fool I say, "Well, I will drive the VW back one time and measure your speed."

I turn around, and with no plan at all about how to do this, we start down the hill. Here is the scene:

Garland starts off behind me, I am gaining speed and I start to think just how stupid this is. I lose sight of Garland's little flashlight he is holding in his hand. Now, where the hell is he? Is he beside the bus or is he very close to the back of the VW? Has he run over the hill?

I am really starting to get skeered that I might run over him. If I touch the brakes I may run over him or he might run into the back of the VW. Then, all of a sudden, I see sparks on the road in front of me. One of Garland's runners has hit one of the very few bare spots on the road.

Somehow Garland has passed me.

I slow down and stop on the bridge. Has Garland ridden his sleigh right under the VW bus? There is no way he could have passed me; I would have seen him come by. So when Garland tells me that he passed me on the right side by going up on the snowbank I am truly relieved.

"But why in the world did you choose to race between the car and snow bank?" I ask.

"I don't know it just looked like fun," he says.

The last time I had the nerve to look was at 26 miles per

hour. I do not have a clue what the top speed was. Some days I wonder how I got to be this old. How did Garland get to be as old as he is?

Bicycles and Bicycles

A few days back, I was riding one of my bicycles and a young man pedaled up beside me and asked me if I had been riding long. I guess my weaving back and forth across the road did not demonstrate all of my true skills. Possibly it was the amount of hard breathing I was doing; he looked at me like I was the main source of air pollution around Pandapas Pond. The truth is, I was kind of weaving and huffing a little. Not that my age and being moderately obese has anything to do with breathing hard. I did answer his question: "Yes, I do ride a little." But it set me to thinking about my bicycle riding over the years.

You see, I once had an old English bicycle. I do not have one clue as to where I got it. Possibly Hubert Grissom found it at VPI after the college students left, and he gave it to me. It was a fine-looking machine, one of those 26- inch bicycles with the very, very narrow tires, a three-speed shifter on the handle bars and a good seat, too. It had a pretty good paint job. There was only one problem with this thing, well two problems really: it would not go, and if it did it would not stop.

First off, it had no sprocket chain. So if I rode it I had to push it, then jump on, then push it again. If you rode it down a hill, you had to push it back up. The other problem was it had no brakes, I mean none. To stop, you either rode the bicycle until the contraption got tired of rolling and quit, or you jumped off. One could always jump over the handle bars. Other than these two shortcomings, it was quite a little jewel.

I must have been at least ten or eleven when I became the owner of the bicycle. Mom and Dad would not let me go anywhere on this thing. Dad said that it was only good for one or two things: "Getting you killed or maimed or even both; and if you come back only maimed I might just finish you off anyway. Don't ride it until you can afford to get that wheel fixed." (Daddy did not call a bicycle a bicycle; he called it a wheel.) So I only rode it the barber shop and back or to Grandmother's; push a while and coast a while.

So being "tough as pine knot and having a head as hard as any of the yellow flint rocks in Shorty's pasture" (Daddy loved to say that), one afternoon when no one was around or looking I pushed the thing over to Sam Smith's. Sam and Helen lived at the very top of Sucker Snider Hill, across the road from the Lytton Cemetery. From their house the next stop was Longs Shop; it was no more than a one-mile downhill grade.

Well, I gave the thing a push, jumped on and down the hill I went. Within two seconds I knew that I was in for one hell of a ride. Within about five seconds I was passing Mod Snyder's, house and I was starting to question doing this. Within six seconds I was passing Gilbert Hilton's house. Aunt Beady Hilton was on the porch, but I don't think she ever saw me. I was just a blur as I passed the house. Within ten seconds I was passing Tommy Pendleton's house. I was moving like a freight train passing a hobo. I knew that I was in trouble!! I mean real trouble.

Just as I was approaching Joe Mack's and Burgess Albert's house, I got to thinking that I just might make it. The luck of youth might be in my favor after all. The hard top is only one very narrow lane wide. As I looked up over the handle bars, I saw my luck running out. Two cars were passing up the hill just past Terry Albert's grandmother's house. For cars to pass, both were required to be off the hard top. That left the ditch for me. There was no place for me to go. I mean no place except turn up one of the driveways. Truly, I had about two seconds to make up my mind what to do. So I stuck both feet right up on the front tire and pushed down hard. I was wearing my old Chuck Taylor Tennis shoes. They were right thin, because they'd been handed down to me. After this day, they were even thinner. They heated up real fast. The friction heat burned into the meat of my foot in less than a second. But I had to keep slowing down. At the very last second, I turned into Joe Mack's driveway and flipped over the handlebars. I hit the road hands first and slid to Burgess' on my forehead.

The cars never even stopped to see if I made it. I can see that Purple Mercury passing me now. I think that it was Boo Boo Hungate, but I am not for sure.

I just lay there on the gravels for a little while. After a few moments I got to my feet. There wasn't a soul anywhere to offer any help. Not one person to help tell the story, either. I managed to pitch the bicycle over the bank into the weeds and slowly walked to Terry's house. Nancy Albert picked the gravels out of my hands and head.

When I got home, no one said a word. Probably Nancy Albert had called Mom and Daddy. I reckon they knew that I learned a lot on this ride, and they could not add much to this lesson. I am sure that they had done things much like this, and they was just remembering how bad their head stung.

Now, it was weeks before my hands healed; I still have the scars and look at them once in a while as a reminder. As for my head, there was a scab larger than a silver dollar for a long time. It took about two weeks for the black eyes to go away and about a month to grow skin over my forehead. To be honest, I think I came very near to being killed. Today, I think the luck of my youth must have been riding on the handlebars after all. This was a great place to be on the Channel 7 news if anyone had owned a TV to watch. I will bet you that I was going more than 15 miles per hour when I hit the road.

The next two-wheeler I bought outright. It was a little bicycle, but it was a whole bicycle. It had 20-inch tires and very high ape-hanger handle bars. It also had coaster brakes. The stroke was so short that it made your legs hurt to pedal. It did not go very fast, but it would stop. I was working on Tommy Adams' Farm in the summer putting up hay and saved up the money to buy the thing brand new from Western Auto in Blacksburg.

One morning I counted up all my money and started walking to town. Blacksburg wasn't more than 10 miles, and I knew that I would get a ride just any minute. I had thumbed to town many times and a ride always came along. On this day, the rides were few and far between. I had walked almost to Prices Fork; I was just about ready to buy a bottle of pop and go back home and put off bicycle-buying until another day. When Leon Sherman picked me up, I told him where I was headed. Leon asked what I was looking for, and I told him that I wanted something with brakes and a sprocket chain. The rest did not matter too much. He said that both were important parts. He also said that maybe I should look around a little bit. This was very sound advice, but I did not take it. I had done made up my mind and did not want to be confused by more facts and information. I did not want options; I just wanted a bicycle.

When I got to Western Auto, I did very little looking at bicycles. I looked at the price tags and found one that I could afford, paid cash and jumped on. I like to have never got that little thing home; it was a son of a bitch to pedal. But it was mine, all mine, bought and paid for with hard-earned cash money. It had a horn on it as big as a road-tractor horn. You could hear it from my house on River Ridge all the way to Long Shop. At this time I could holler like Tarzan, too. I would blow that horn a time or two and whoop. I did this just to let everyone know that I was on my way.

I would ride to Long Shop and push that little bike back up the Sucker Snider Hill. As I passed each house, people would ask me why I didn't ride it home. I just kept pushing. I have no idea where the little bike went, but good riddance. It made my knees ache trying to pedal the thing. I should have taken Leon's advice. Just remember that he probably had a bicycle also, and if I had listened my knees would not have hurt. But he was too old to know very much, and I was too young to know how to listen.

The old English bicycle and the little green spider bike were not my only ventures into two-wheel transportation. I was working on the farm at Whitethorn with Chuck Shorter when I bought a used bicycle from Reynard Hale, Superintendent of Montgomery County Schools. I was most likely about 22 or 23 years old. I was living most of the time at the cabin on the river, when I wasn't mooching off of Mom and Dad. One could always find me at their house on Monday night watching the football game, for sure. This bike was the exact opposite of the English one. I think this one was called an "American Bicycle." It did have a sprocket chain and coaster brakes. Sounds pretty good so far, doesn't it? Another neat difference was the tires. This one had tires that looked a whole lot like a set of VW tires, big and wide. I would ride this behemoth to work some days, but

I was not man enough to do it every day. I needed a day's rest between rides. That thing was giant. I would ride it to work, and Chuck would be nice enough to take me home.

Everything went very well for a few weeks. Then one day I was riding to work after lunch. I was crossing the road fill just behind Sam Smith's house, when the front axle broke. Yes, it just snapped in two, and in much less than a heartbeat the front fork dug right into the hardtop. Everything just came to a stop real quick. But, to my surprise, I just picked up my feet as my momentum thrust me forward, stepped over the handlebars and jogged to a stop. Not one scratch. I walked back to pick up all of the pieces and pitched them over the road fill. I guess the locusts and the blackberry briars have eaten away that rascal, one piece at a time by now.

I turned to the very next car and stuck out my thumb. Mrs. Roberts (who knew me) stopped, and I jumped in. I immediately noticed that she was looking uncomfortable. She let me out at the road to Whitethorn. As I walked and jogged back to the farm, I pondered her reaction to me. Now I had had onions and hot dogs for lunch, but I do not think that was it. Possibly it could have been the corn silage we had been working in that morning. Who knows? I was in a phase of poor hygiene, so that could have done it too. Maybe it was all three smells. I honestly do not know how Chuck Shorter took it. He did, and we remain friends to this day. I guess Poor Old Chuck's nose is not working. One of these days, when I work up the nerve, I may ask Mrs. Roberts about that short ride.

I bought a 10-speed when I was going to school at The University of Rhode Island. I rode that thing everywhere. Either I was right tough, or the land was mostly flat. I do not know which it was, but me and the machine did log a lot of miles up and down the hurricane escape road from Point Judith to Narragansett. I could ride it holding a surf-fishing rod and bait can. Now that was something to see. When I left URI (University of Rhode Island) and headed for the University of Tennessee at Martin, I took it with me.

We had an older VW then. It was loaded heavily and was slow. I had the bicycle on top of the car. The tires were tied up with a hay string holding them so they would not turn. Down the road we came, the CB turned up loud. That was the only way you could hear it over the car noises. Somewhere in Pennsylvania, I heard one of the truckers laughing at my bicycle. One driver was explaining to another that if the VW slowed down any more, he expected me to jump out, flip the car over and pedal the VW over the next hill. A third driver chimed in that he'd seen just such a thing happen.

Well, I will tell you this, that old 10-speed did like West Tennessee just like Rhode Island. It was flatter than a pancake out there. I never wrecked the thing very much, just a few cuts and a bruised ego a few times. I was just saving up for later.

One morning, when I was about 40 years old, I woke up on my own again. I had no clue what to do or where to go to do it. I just wandered around kind of like a lost ball in the high weeds for a while, until one day I was driving past Corning

Glass Works and walked into a used sporting goods store.

In an instant, all of the lost pieces fell back into place. There was a used bicycle. A little cream puff with most of the paint worn off and bald tires. Yes, there sat an old Bridgestone Bicycle with a steel frame, and it weighed a little less than a ton. Hell, the thing even looked like me. And, holy macaroni, it was just like buying the little green spider bike 25 years earlier. I looked at the price tag and never blinked. I rolled it to the cash register, flat tires and all, and said, "I'll take it." I opened my billfold, and there was not money enough to purchase the little cream puff. A little dose of reality set in, and I offered the man what I had. He said, "Sold!"

My outlook on the world changed overnight. Off to the mountain I went, and I mean I had a ball! I eventually got two new tires and had the thing tuned up real good. As I gained proficiency on this Mountain Bike, I got to thinking that when Ponce de Leon was looking for the Fountain of Youth, he simply looked in the wrong place. The Fountain of Youth had handlebars and 28 little gears on it all fixed up for climbing hills. Up hills were hard, but downhill took care it itself. I bet I wrecked it 25 times without hurting me or messing up the bike too much. Then, one day, I jumped over a log and mashed the back wheel. I could not ride it out of the mountain. I had to carry it more than seven miles, all of the way from Kettle Rock Hole to the upper parking lot at Pandapas Pond. I took it straight to the bike shop and said, "Fix it." Before the night was over. Little Man Jack had made up a special wheel for it, one with

36 spokes. Yes, 36 spokes. It looked much like a spider web back there and had its own kind of hum when it went downhill. But it would not bend with my full eighth of ton on it, no sir. She was now a true Mountain Bike, and since I was the owner I must now have become a true mountain biker or something like that.

On Saturday morning, I picked up Hugo Roberts, and we went to the mountains. On this new wheel and with new gears set much lower, this thing was a true climber. Add in a new clean sprocket chain, and I was flat out ready. Hills and flat stretches did not have a chance. I had truly arrived at my pinnacle of pedaling power. I was a middle-aged force, or some may say a middle-aged fool, to be reckoned with for sure. I sure wish you could have seen me. Believe it or not, I even started riding the mountains with people much younger than myself, and I could keep up. Some I even passed!

Back to the story — I just came down a hill on Poverty Creek and started out a flat stretch with that little cream puff. I was pedaling for all I was worth. That back wheel was just a humming like a jar fly. I was a bone-headed, 45-year-old man looking for his youth. I let the front tire reach down into a very low trench. It was not more than 10 inches deep and six or seven inches wide. I was still pedaling for all the good Lord would give me. In retrospect, I am glad the Good Lord did not give me any more.

My left foot pedal touched the top of the trench on the down stroke. In less than a second, the bicycle was picked up, and over the handlebars I went. The first part of me that land-ed was my chest; somehow my hands were behind me. Hugo said that I must have traveled more than 10 feet in the air be-fore I landed. I slid another 10 or 15 feet before I came to rest. I rolled over; I truly thought that I would never walk again. My chest and ribs hurt so bad that I did not see or feel the cuts on my knees and arms. Hugo offered very little encouragement. "Come on, get up. I have a date," he said. He could not just leave me, because we were riding in my little green truck. I got up and pushed the thing back to the truck. Dr. McCone said I had only broken three ribs. Somehow they were broken in the front of my sternum.

Later, as I told my story, people just shook their heads. In the next few weeks I had the bicycle straightened out and back on the road. I was not able to ride it much or breathe deeply without pain. I have learned the human body is one tough thing. It was months before I could ride fast or even run without my chest hurting. Also coughing was a life-changing experience. But that is another story.

Well, one day, off again I went—bicycle shopping. This time I did my homework and finally took Leon Sherman's ad-vice, some 25 years too late. I wanted a strong, lightweight steel frame. I wanted a shock absorber fork and a set of pulling gears that would permit me to climb a tree if I so chose. I bought a Univega Alpina 505. I would buy it all over again just for the name. It is as light as a feather. Possibly, that is why it liked to fly so much. Well, I found it, and it did everything one could ever ask of it. You just could not stop the hard-headed thing.

I still have the Alpina, and I look at it right often, but don't ride it much. Truly, the only problem with the thing is that it is much faster and more athletic than I am. You see, it is just a little shorter in length than the others; it is also a might higher off of the ground. It is very maneuverable. A better way to say it is the Alpina is more of a man than I am. Now I have only had two really memorable wrecks on the thing. Well, two that I want you to know about. But, there have been many more minor ones. Oh, yes, many more. Remind me to tell you about the time I landed on the top of a small oak tree.

It is the dead of winter and the road is icy. Now about every rednecked boy I know has something programmed into him that compels him to go to Mountain Lake when it snows. Me, too, I go about every time; I simply cannot help it. On this particular day, I start out for Little Meadows, not in my truck nor am I walking; I am riding that Alpina on the slick road.

The gravel road had very long stretches of white ice. Then for a ways there would be stretches of gravel. I have my lunch in a little backpack and a bottle of water. I am going out for the day, I think; I am headed for the fire tower. I am taking my time. When the front tire slips on one of the ice packs, I just lean into the slide, and old Teddy (that's my bicycle's nickname) comes right back up.

Looked like a true pro, I did. This was a piece of cake. The next time the front tire broke traction, I did the same thing, and it came back up again. By now, I was about 9 or 10 miles back in the mountain, not too far from the fire tower. I was moving on pretty good, but possibly a little too fast. The front tire lost traction, I leaned into it, and the bicycle just kept going.

The wild thing just flipped over. I do not mean a big slide or anything like that; I mean it flipped over. The right side of my head was the first thing that hit the ice. It happened so fast that my shoes were still hooked to the pedals. Note, I said my head not my helmet. I have a real good helmet; it just happened to be in the truck. I truly saw stars, and I got real sick to my stomach. I also had a pounding headache. I did manage to get the bicycle back up on the road. Now, I was as cold as I have ever been, even though the temperature was well up around 35 to 40 degrees. I was very light-headed and dizzy, then sick again.

I could not ride the bicycle. So I just started pushing it back to the truck. Over the next four or five hours I spent more time getting dizzy and being sick feeling and leaning on the bicycle than walking. I went slowly, because of the pounding headache. Every time I speeded up, my head pounded even more. Walk, set down, be sick—all of the way back. Since I could not eat that fine lunch, I carried it back to the truck, too.

It was near dark by the time I reached the truck, and by the time I got home I was starting to get some better. Better is a relative term here; I was truly sick and did not know just how bad until later. But, to say the least, I did not ride any more until the road melted off. The bad headache went away, and the ice melted about the same time.

It took about three weeks to get everything back to normal. I was afraid to go to the medical doctor for fear of what the rascal would tell me. So, I just took lots of aspirin and slept a lot. If you're a true red-necked boy, you always self-treat before you let a doctor have crack at you!

When spring came, me and the Alpina gave each other another chance. I loved parking at the bottom of the road leading to the Audie Murphy Monument. As I said earlier, that Alpina loves to climb, and I like to watch it go. It is truly a hoss. I was still young enough to love feeling my heart beat hard. On a good climb, you can maybe hear the blood running through your ears; I just like that. Sometimes I could hear it over the crunching of the gravels, and my breathing like there was no tomorrow.

From the hardtop at the bottom of the mountain to the monument is probably no more than a five-mile climb. For a true masculine Appalachian Specimen like me, it takes a while to get there. I am guessing about 90 minutes. So, I still pedal uphill slowly. But on the return, I turn Old Teddy loose. I am just flying back down the hill, cruising just under the speed of sound and running before the wind. I love to stand high up on the pedals and use my body to gain wind resistance to slow down. I like the feel of the air on me. I like to feel the sweat being dried off of me too. It feels kind of like setting on the top of a hay wagon as you make your way to the barn, only better.

Just for few seconds I lose my concentration on what I am doing. Somehow I let my momentum pull me too far to the outside of a turn. Here the gravels are piled up right thick. I just cannot get the bicycle straightened back up in the soft gravels. So, at an extremely fast rate of speed, I go over the bank. I fly through the air a short distance, but my momentum carries me a far piece. I ride down probably an acre of weeds, blackberry briars, and many, many young locust and sumac trees. I come to rest very hard, on a great big sandstone about the size of my pickup truck. One thing for sure, I do a whole lot more sliding on my head, chest, back, arms and belly than flying. Thank goodness there are a lot of blackberry briars and small locust trees to slow me down before the big rock. No helmet on again; far too hot for wearing a helmet.

The bicycle comes to rest way out in a pasture. How it got over or under the American Wire Fence is beyond me. I don't care much, either. The main thing is I have not run headfirst into the fence. Why, at my speed, I might have got myself cut into about 50 little six-inch squares. If I had hit that fence at high speed, the little squares of me would have had to be stacked up and glued back together. Also, thank the Lord for the very large sandstone. It just might have been the only thing that saved me.

From the way I feel, I know I am broke up inside in more places than I could name. If I had a cell phone, I would call for The Prices Gulf to bring their wrecker, the big one, to get me back up the hill and an ambulance to carry me off somewhere. After a while I manage to roll over on my back. That is not as easy as you might think, being all broke up inside and all scratched up outside. Somehow, I lay my hand right on my eye glasses and start looking me over. Place by place, I go over me. I am so happy to find no place broken, but there is no place that isn't bruised, scratched and kind of seeping blood. I am not dripping too much blood, but there is plenty enough for the gnats to get stuck in and worry me.

I do not see any bones sticking out of the skin anywhere. This is my second trip through the blackberry briars and small locust trees; it should teach me something. I need to get out of the woods! I am torn up, scratched up and hurting. I crawl under the fence out into the field and rescue my bicycle. I do not have the heart or strength to pitch it back over the fence, so we just walk through the field for a while.

When I finally get to the road and walk around a little, I can tell I am not broke up as bad as I had thought. Appalachian boys are tough, real tough. Not too smart, just awful tough.

Yes, I still have the Alpina 505 and still like to say its name— "Alpina." Don't ride it much anymore. You see, the cost of Band-Aids has gone up and all. Maybe I am just a little scared of it, too. One of these days I am going to look up what Alpina means; I can just bet it means: "You are going to get scratched up and bruised." What do you think?

After this experience, I put that thing up on a nail in the garage. I went and bought me a Lemond road bike. It is named after Greg Lemond, the famous American bicycle rider. He was one of the earlier American Tour de France winners. So you know it had to be a good one. And I started riding the Blue Ridge Parkway. This bike has three gears on the crank and six gears on the back wheel. I can even pedal it up hills right easily. At least, if you wreck there is somebody coming by after a while. I also now wear a helmet.

It was on one of my trips down the Blue Ridge Parkway that I learned the importance of a bicycle helmet. Miss Gail and me are out for one of our many short trips (I would like someday to ride from Cherokee, NC, to Washington, DC.), and I am just riding along trying to mind my own business when out of nowhere a very nice, shiny car comes by me just one or two miles per hour faster than me. The car is so close that his mirror almost knocks me off the Greg Lemond. I jerk the bicycle hard to the right, and down over a steep grassy hill I go. I am flipped over the handlebars and land squarely on my head. No harm done to either me or the bicycle. But my neck was very stiff. Without the helmet, who knows? Miss Gail might have never found me until the buzzards took to circling.

I did learn that you always need to have your eyes open for town boys. They like to play rough and drive off in their shiny cars. A country boy would have pulled the same trick. The difference is a country boy would have stopped to ask if I was hurt. Then he would have took to laughing and drove off!

The Greg Lemond now spends a lot time in the garage up on a nail, too.

Well, this might seem like a right long answer to that boy's question. I just wanted you to get the full benefit of what I've learned. Most of my riding has been a pretty bad experience, but I am just hoping to get the hang of it one day. If you want to see the Univega Alpina 505 and the Lemond, they are both hanging up in the garage. These days they don't appear to be going anywhere very fast. I do try to keep the tires pumped up and their sprocket chains oiled. It is just my way of trying to keep my memory of being more youthful and being a bicycle rider. Come on by and look at them if you want to; they ain't going nowhere.

Gail said that I could have a traumatic head injury if I was to wreck too much. She doesn't know the half of what this old head has had happen to it. I am somewhat reluctant to write it all down, for she might someday want me to visit a real doctor and have it looked into or something.

OtherThings
with Wheels

The truth is there were other things with wheels that used to amuse us boys on River Ridge when we weren't fishing, swimming, hunting, eating or putting up hay. In its divine wisdom, when The Great State of Virginia built the new road to Long Shop, it left the very steep section of the road from Sam Smith's to Carson Whitaker's with nothing to do but just lay there. We boys of Long Shop took it upon ourselves to use that piece of unwanted road and that almost forgotten hill.

Now, speaking just for me here, I could not build a rock pile. So I sure could not build a coaster wagon. They were a cross between a soapbox derby car, Radio Flyer Wagon, an old lawn mower, a wheelbarrow and a two-wheel dolly used at the feed store. Scientifically speaking, they were a hybrid machine of our own invention and our own design. Very complicated machines they were. I sure put a lot of time into trying to learn to build mine! Mostly I was learning what not to do.

About everyone I can think of in and around Long Shop or River Ridge made one of the things. No two of the contraptions looked alike either, though all the while they were about the same design. All one needed was four wheels. If you were one of the lucky boys, you had four wheels all the same size. Then, if you were even luckier, they were all the same kind. That did not happen very often unless you came across an old unused lawn mower. Some of the time we just borrowed lawn mower wheels when no one was mowing. Sometimes contestants brought hybrid machines for testing, too — you know, ones with a set of mixed-sized wheels.

Here is what was required to build one of these contraptions. You needed a total of three boards, two pieces of concrete reinforcement bar and four wheels. The one 2x8 needed to be about eight feet long. Two 2x4s should be at least four feet long. The length of boards would vary according to what you could scrounge up. Construction was simple. You nailed a 2x4 across the back of your 2x8 to create a rear axle mounting, then nailed the re-bar to the rear 2x4 and added two wheels.

In the front you nailed an axle, also, plus two more wheels. Here is where it got a little tricky. You see, you set on the thing and steered with your feet. So, you just attached the front 2x4 with only one big nail so that it could pivot. I just never thought about a bolt with a lock nut to hold my front axle. I just never did. That one step would have saved lots of Mom's Merthiolate. Another thing that people tended to forget was a long piece of rope tied onto the front. This was important for dragging the thing out of the weeds and pulling it back up the Sucker Snider Hill. I think you kind of get the picture. I am thinking you got a real safe picture in your mind, too. The contraptions never did last as long as the scratches and the Merthiolate marks did.

When we got going, we just gave that thing a push off of the hill up by the Lytton Cemetery, and down the hill we went. At the bottom of the hill, if you did not wreck first, you jumped off before the intersection with the new road. Getting off often meant hitting a road ditch or running over the bank into the weeds and blackberry briars. This may not sound like much to you, but at eight or nine miles per hour, it was quite a jolt. After a dozen trips you were well aware that the ditch and bank were just full of blackberry briars, broken liquor bottles and small locust trees, beer bottles and weeds, a dead opossum or two and little pieces of your skin. Upon hitting the ditch, within one second you were literally stabbed and poked all over.

Very often, for me, it did require a trip home where Mom would stretch me over a picnic table in the backyard and pick out most of the splinters and fill each hole with Merthiolate. Mom knew that would burn real bad, and she liked seeing me squirm. Sometimes she would say: "One of these days you are going to catch rabies or come home with something really bad; you just wait and see."

Now, if you wrecked on the asphalt before you made it to the ditch, you were scratched and skinned up unmercifully. One time, while attending Blacksburg High School, a few local boys and me saw a boy fall and skin his leg on the basketball floor. He took to limping and squirming. We looked at each other and said, "Hell, he needs to hit the hardtop in front of Carson Whitaker's just once, that will show him what a skinned place looks like."

But it was fun. I went to Lakeside Amusement Park down in Salem once, and I did not see one thing that could equal jumping off at Carson Whitaker's. I saw nothing that took that much nerve, either.

I had a friend, whose name I'd better not mention, who brought one of the contraptions to the hill one morning. It was the envy of the group, with a strong-looking center board and two good-looking lawn mower wheels on the front. The back wheels caught my attention. He had two 12-inch iron wheels on the back. the kind you often saw on old wheelbarrows and two-wheel carts at the feed store. Yes sir, this thing was built for speed. When he took off down the hill, he was truly getting it. You could measure his speed by the iron wheels clicking. Then there was a bunch of muffled hollers, lots of oh's, and expletives. I was behind him on my contraption; I kind of saw it all. I felt for him. The iron wheels did not stick to the road real good. When he tried to steer, they just started to slide. Well, I knew what was next for him. He needed the needle for picking out splinters and gravels and the bottle of Merthiolate.

I do think that these life experiences should be enough to at least make me look at situations with both eyes. Well, it has some of the time.

DOWN BY

THE RIVER

The Creek

From the time I can remember I just wanted to go to the river. Even when I was in high school and older I wanted to take everyone to the Bus. Even today, I can think about the river and a million stories just come flooding back into my mind.

But, before I was turned loose on the river, I had to master being turned loose on the creek. Tom's Creek was a short walk from my home on River Ridge. I just had to walk though Mr. Luther Snyder's pasture out behind his barn, crawl under the fence in the ditch and walk through Maury Long's woods and through one more pasture to the creek. It was no more than a mile or so. I cannot tell you how many hours I spent around the creek. I was there day and night, all four seasons.

Mom and Dad first let me start going to the creek by myself when I was about 6 or 7 years old. By then, though, I had slipped off many times before. I had the path wore clean and wide. I was hardheaded and was going anyway. I figured that they just gave in and turned me loose. It was just better than wondering which way I had gone. Mom said that at the ripe old age of one, or when every baby starts talking, my very first word that they could make out was "outside." The way she remembered it, I would pull up to a window and stand looking outside. I have not been back inside until recently.

I think that spending so much time in and around Tom's Creek just made me want to go to New River even more. Almost every evening, I could be found setting on "Fuzzy" Norris's foot-bridge. Sometimes Mom or Dad would holler down over the hill telling me it was time to come home. Every once in awhile Dad would drive over and pick me up. He never once got out of the panel wagon — excuse me, out of the Suburban — to join me. I know that he used to go to the creek when he was a youngster, too. I reckon he just forgot about it.

I could and did sit there on the creek bank for hours on end watching fish, lizards, crawfish and swarms of insects. Once in a while, I even fished. Often I caught a chub or two and a few redeyes. It was rare that I caught enough fish to take home. But, you could float a fresh-caught grasshopper or bee down through the brush and always catch something.

One of the best things about these trips to the creek was the quiet. You hardly ever saw anyone. Back then, once in awhile a car would pass. Sometimes I would see some of the other kids out on the creek. I always was fishing for fun. One of them kids once told me that he was fishing for supper. It always seemed like they could use an extra meal or two.

One very late August day, I was setting on the footbridge. As usual, if I looked in the water right close, I could see little fish of every description. The water was very clear and low. In the still pools, some leaves with a little bit of color were starting to collect, and there was summer dust floating on top of the water. The season was changing, and I was totally unaware of it. I felt like these days would last forever. Time seems to move slowly for an eight-year-old. I followed the creek from one deep pool to another. I had spent a lot of my time just sitting around when I wasn't working. Well, Dad called down over the hill for me to come to the footbridge. I bet that the Simmonses, the Wilsons and the Norrises got tired of all that hollering.

It was time for Mom and Dad to take me to Pembroke, and get me some new shoes. Yes, the season was changing all right. It was time for school, and I was totally unaware of this. I might have been just suppressing the misery of thinking about setting in that hot classroom thinking about stuff other than fishing and of places I had never heard of. I know that this isn't very exciting, but another summer was gone and was never ever coming back.

While I was waiting for Daddy and the rest of the family, I thought back to the last pair of shoes and where in the heck had this summer gone. I got a new pair of shoes every fall. They would be a little too big in the beginning, and when I threw them out of the school bus window the next spring, they would be almost foot-hurting small. Sometimes, I was given a new pair of steel-toed safety shoes from the Radford Arsenal. I always appreciated them, but I knew that Daddy was still wearing old ones, so that I could have better ones. They never did fit very well either, but you just wore what you had.

I guess the old shoes had served me well. I once knew a boy, only a little older than me, who came to school barefooted. I asked Mom if I could go to school without shoes. Mom would just say no. Dad would tell me not to be making fun of people that don't have money for shoes. I guess you could tell I was a little better off, because my feet were all pinched and hurting, and I had on shoes just a little too small for my feet. But, I had shoes.

As the idea of school started to creep in on me, I thought about the past summer. I took to thinking about the fish I had seen and caught and other neat things, too. The fish were in the deeper pools, and I troubled myself over where the best grasshoppers were. I gave careful thought to where the fewest snakes might be. Mostly I thought about swimming naked in the creek. Skinny-dipping is the best kind of swimming. I even thought that the time I was caught swimming naked. Once during the summer a young lady, daughter of one of the local families, not more than 11 or 12, caught me skinny-dipping. I grabbed my clothes and ran like I was on fire. When I went back, she said she would not tell anyone. Now that I am 55 or 56 years old and thinking back, I guess I could have asked her to join me. A year or so later, I learned that one of the local men had been real mean to her. She just went away, and I did not see much of her after that.

I even thought about honeybees. Mr. John Amos had 10 or 15 honeybee hives just below the Johnny (The Fox) Simpsons' barn. If I was lucky, I would be taking one of my surveys of the creek when Mr. Amos would be checking his beehives. He would always let me watch and help. I thought it was great when I got to wear his bee mask and big gloves. I don't think that I ever got stung, either. Mr. Amos was never stung when he came to take the honey supers off. Sometimes we just took off the supers and looked at the honeycombs. We just wanted to see if the bees had been working or spending their summer being lazy. He would look at me and chuckle. I think that he thought that I had spent my summer being lazy, and that his wife, Old Mrs. Amos, would soon get that out of me. Mrs. Amos taught school at Prices Fork Elementary School, and she was as tough and strict as they come. She would never harm a hair on your head, but she was really good at busying your butt with a real big paddle. Yessir, she was good with that paddle. Mrs. Amos always came to our family reunions. She went to others, too. She was a great lady!

Mr. Amos told me to be nice to creatures and people, and they will always be nice to you. I never told him that I would catch as many of the little stinging rascals as I could. I used many of his bees for fish bait when the grasshoppers were hard to catch. The perch seemed to like them.

As I have gotten older, I think I was born at the very end of the "Little Ice Age" that teachers now talk about in school. Once upon a time way back when, it did get cold and stay cold. Anyway that was before Al Gore was thinking up the meaning of "Global Warming."

Just because it got cold and everything froze over, that

did not stop you from going to the creek. Prior to the creek freezing, we walked the creek banks looking for fish big enough to gig. Often it was just Terry and me. Sometimes Old Butter Bean would join us; he would take the fish home and eat them. One time Terry gigged a right small fish and was about to pitch him back. Butter Bean said: "Give him to me. He is big enough to put on a biscuit." So he took that one home, as well. Once Butter Bean said that one time when he was on his way home from gigging the game warden stopped his car to offer him a ride. We asked, "What did he say about the gigged fish you were carrying?" Butter Bean said, "I had put them in my pockets so the game warden wouldn't see them." Good hiding place. I would never have thought of that.

Another good way to catch fish in the creek was with cherry bombs. All you had to do was find you a hole with fish big enough to eat, light the cherry bomb and pitch it in the water. When it went off, it would stun the fish and you could pick them up before they got themselves straightened out. This way I, too, could have fish for breakfast. We only took the big suckers and redeyes. The rest we let swim off.

When it did get cold and everything froze over, we still went to the creek. Terry Albert and I would walk the frozen banks. Often the ice would be 6 or 7 inches thick. We were still going fishing. I guess it was ice fishing, Long Shop style. Neither of us knew exactly how they did it in other places.

Our method was simple. You just carried an ax with you. When you saw a good fish, one up near the bottom of the ice, you walked out onto the ice real slow. Then you rared back and hit the ice with the blunt end of the ax just over the fish. It would stun the fish for a few minutes. Then you walked to the next melted-out riffle and waited for the fish to float out.

The only drawback to this kind of fishing was getting wet and cold. Sometimes you'd have to wade out up to your knees or more to pick up your fish. I had no clue what the temperature was and did not care. It did not seem to bother us much. Most of the fish we caught were hog suckers and once in awhile a bass.

It was worth it! I would take my fish home on a stick through their gills or in a small paint bucket and clean and scale them outside on an old table. Then I would take them in the house to wash them right good. The next morning when Mom had time, she would have a frying pan with good fresh lard sizzling. She dipped the fish in an egg batter then rolled them in flour and cornmeal. Next she laid that fish in the pan. When they got crispy all around, I would eat like the true and rightful King of all River Ridge. I can think of no one who ever ate better. Some mornings, Mom would roll slices of eggplant in that batter and fry them with the fish. That was good eating, too. Dad said that was the way they ate fish in the city. I thought that city life might not be all that bad. Hogsuckers may be bony and hard to clean, but they were sure good to eat.

My Day Finally Came!

When I got a little older, Mom gave in and let me start going to the river by myself. And, about this time, Bobby Lee "Rock" Henson -- that was Hap Henson's grandson -- started joining me as an official sack setter or a fourth person in the boat.

Rock and I asked if we could take a turn in the gigging boat. We had asked many times before, but the answer always came back "no." To our delight the answer this time was "yes." Hell, a new day in fish-gigging had just begun. The river was starting to dingy up a little. And, the gigging light was starting to weaken, but we did it. I will bet that me and Rock gigged four or five nights a week after that. I got to looking pale like Old Boo Radley. I slept most of the day and gigged all night. A big fish did not have a chance. And the little ones took to running as soon as they heard us dipping the boat out.

It was about this time that Terry Albert and Chuck Shorter entered my circle of friends, and we launched a whole new generation of fish-gigging. As for me, I think I became the best boat-poler I ever saw. Since Mod Snider, Harry Graham, Boyd McCann and Gilbert Hilton are not here to vote, I simply win by default. Now, they were very good. Any of them could move a boat across the river and never make a riffle. I offer a quiet word of grace in respect for the skill they showed for this job! They were good.

The Old Paddle

Let me tell you about the big riffle at Lover's Leap. This is the place where the river grew narrow, and the water got to moving real fast. One of my most impressive riverboat skills was exhibited in this very riffle. For a while, this feat of true New River skill was talked about down at the store. Well, I talked about it a lot. Some listened; some didn't. I did like the story. Still do.

Often men would just get out of their boat and struggle to pull it over this riffle. I could paddle a boat up and through it. Once, when Daddy and I were at Byrd Sheppard's sawmill, he spied a piece of poplar about two inches thick by ten inches wide and ten feet long. There wasn't a flaw in the board. We brought it home and went over to Mr. Luther Snider's house. Mr. Luther was a woodworker of great renown. Together, we cut out the perfect boat paddle. What made this one so special was that it had a three-foot blade and a handle so long that it required the operator to be standing. "Why, no one but you would want such a thing. A paddle like that would kill any ordinary man," Daddy and Mr. Luther laughed.

If you put your heart into working this paddle, you could move mountains. In other words, if you was tough enough to stay with it, you could paddle up the Lover's Leap Riffle. I learned that all you had to do was come to the riffle from the Radford Arsenal side and keep to the shallow side to paddle through. My heart beat very fast afterwards, but that was ok. I could rest later. I was on my way to the burning ground and them big flat rocks with the deep channels.

The Radford Arsenal people had stretched a big cable across the river to mark the boundary between Public River and Government River. The government was very picky about what they owned, and they let you know it. I was still too young to vote, so I did not holler back at them too awful much when they would run me out.

For the most part, a feller could not pass beyond the cable. Sometimes the arsenal guard would let me pass and paddle on up near the burning grounds. Sometimes he would holler and tell me that I had gone far enough. Other times I would just pass the guard tower and never hear a word. The guard rascal wasn't in the guard tower all the time. He had to sleep sometime or go home once in awhile, and I knew it. Yes, I was a slow learner then, but I was constant. You almost had to try for it every day to catch the guard off duty. It was worth it, because there was real good fishing upriver beyond the cable. Plus, after paddling upwards of two miles against the current with that big paddle, I thought I needed to fish upstream as a kind of reward or something. As I would sneak past the cable I felt like I was part of that story I once read about the Big Two-Hearted River.

In my early life, there was no greater feeling than to paddle above Lover's Leap after the midnight whistle had sounded. Everybody for miles around would be asleep except me. When I have shared this adventure with people in the past, they've looked at me like they thought they were hearing a tall tale. I think they must have just lived a very bland youth.

The night air was most always cool and clean. Often the stars were clear and bright, too. Never was there ever another person on the river. I'd paddle to Lover's Leap, strip off my clothes, jump in the river and swim or float behind the boat as I worked my way back to the bus or the cabin. There was no sound but the noise of water slapping up on the boat and an occasional fish jumping. Once in awhile, when a loud coal train would go up the mountain, I could even feel the vibration in the water. There is no other way to express it; the river was good to me and it seemed like it had a lot to offer.

The Bus

Before the cabin, there was the bus. Yes, the bus. The year was 1966. Mod Snider and Hubert Grissom had built small cinderblock cabins on New River. We did not have one. We had a place, though. The problem was money. You see, I had two brothers and two sisters. With seven mouths to feed, even with the garden and fresh meat, the grocery bill must have been almighty high. Look at me — I do not think that I missed many meals?

One Saturday morning Daddy loaded me up in the VW bus and took me over to Plum Creek. We drove down over a little hill, and there sat an old school bus in a man's back yard. I will never forget Elmer saying, "Well, what do you think? Want to take it to the Whiterock and make a cabin out of it?"

My reply was simple: "Oh, hell yes, but it ain't got any motor in it and no tires. How in the world will you get it there?"

Over the next two or three weekends, we jacked up the old thing, put wheels on it, dug the soil out from under it and made a trailer hitch. One day Chuck Shorter and Jimmy Bland came with us, and all four of us were up under the bus doing something. I think we were taking off the drive shaft. Anyway, I had a bad case of flatulence come over me. Yes, I had gas, and I can just bet you know what came next. Before I tell that part, let me tell you that Daddy, that was Elmer, had a very low tolerance for farts.

I let one of the largest silent farts that ever was. Daddy jumped and hit his head on the bus's frame and squirmed; then he took to cussing. "You damn fartmonger of a son of a bitch," he yelled. Chuck and Jimmy started to laugh uncontrollably and loudly. I just ran like a fool.

I set on the Plum Creek Bridge for a long time. To be honest, I was very embarrassed, and I was right mad at Daddy for cussing me in front of my friends. I could still hear them laughing. Some of the time, I could not stop laughing either. Slowly, I did come back, but I tried not to let on that I was right embarrassed. You see, my social skills were still in the developmental stage and not coming along real well at all.

After all the gas cleared, we bolted on wheels. Mod Snider came over one morning, and we connected the old bus to the back of his dump truck. We started the next day— I think it was a Saturday morning just before daylight. Moving the bus had to be done before any traffic started and on a day when the Radford Arsenal work traffic was low. With this jack-legged operation, there did not need to be too many cars on the road.

Mod started out real slow; I mean real slow. Once the bus moved out a little, Daddy opened the rear end and filled it with heavy oil. I had never heard a thing squeak as much as this thing. In the beginning, the back wheels would not turn. Mod would drive forward a little, then he would back up a little. Nothing seemed to help. After a few early-morning sips of Old Kessler, the men were ready, even if the bus wasn't. They pulled out onto Route 11 and headed east, crawling about three to four miles an hour. By the time the old bus reached the hardtop, the tires had reluctantly started to turn over and they just kept on rolling. The caravan turned left up over the hill on the Plum Creek Road. Mod Snider's speed was never greater than two or three miles per hour. Now the fun started. The road wasn't much wider than the bus and truck. At the time, it was a one-lane gravel road with a lot of pull-offs. Every once in a while, we would stop and let the bearings cool off and take another sip of Kessler. By the time the Kessler was running low, the bus and truck were running well. We squealed and rattled to River Ridge.

We turned the old bus down the road next to Nelson's hog pen and crawled down into the hollow past the potato patch to the railroad. It was time to let everything cool off. Everyone looked at the bus and the hanging electrical wires, and pondered how to get under them. It was decided that we could stand in the bed of the truck with a gig and hold the wires up one at a time, while we towed the bus under. Today, no one but a crazy man would even dream of trying such a thing. There were a few sparks, but not one person got electrified. Not one. This was one time when I was told to "Get the hell away from here," I did just that.

After we cleared the wires, Mod eased the old thing down to the edge of the river and very slowly backed it to its new resting place. Now, I will be honest with you; I thought it was about the best and prettiest thing I had ever seen. I was happier than any boy around. The grown men opened a full brand new bottle of Old Kessler. Another piece of honesty: without the Old Kessler, I do not think the bus would have made the trip. Heck, I would have worked on the old thing for years to have seen it resting at the Whiterock. Every hour would have been worth it. So go on and enjoy the Old Kessler, I thought. I can take it from here.

It was fixed real nice. We put a one-inch plywood floor in it and used plywood to replace the broken windows. We jacked it up and leveled it with cinderblocks and crossties. A very small cinderblock flue was built, and a small two-eyed stove —"A Ginger Glass Glow Stove," no less — was put in for heat and small cooking. It was so small that we had to cut very small pieces of wood for the firebox. Golly, everything was great. In the beginning, before electric lights, we used coal oil lamps. Sometime later we got electricity. I understood just how happy the mountain people were when rural electrification came to the mountains.

From somewhere, four antique double beds appeared.

They were the kind with the tall metal headboards and three-foot-tall footboards, all of which we hack-sawed off to make three of them fit inside. There was not room for the fourth, so it stayed outside as an extra sleeping space.

In the summer, I most often used the outdoor bed. Sleeping there by the river, listening to fish jump and the trains, was simply wonderful. The noise of the insects in the woods came alive when I slept on the outside bed.

For the most part, I was the main bus user, me and my friends. In the future Melvin and Kevin would assume their rightful place as keepers of the bus. Oleta also had a soirée or two there herself. The bus was used as a launching place for all river-related activities. It was also the place where we drank lots of beer and cooked lots of food. Me, I learned a lot about growing up and friendship. What a time and what a place!

The old bus has been gone for more than 20 years, washed away by a river flood and pushed over the bank. But you ask anyone, even people who have never been there, where the old bus is, and you will get exact directions. The Old Bus was just part of life on New River! Even today, 30 years later, people I do not know at all tell of their experiences "At the Bus." It was a hell of a place!

The Crosstie Cabin

All of the boys up and down the river had their special little hideouts, or as we called them, "cabins." Me, I had the bus up at the Whiterock. Chuck Shorter had the log cabin on the creek. It was a converted chicken house that still stands today. But, I personally think that Terry Albert had the most unique little abode of us all.

Terry had a cabin built out of crossties. Yes, crossties -- you know, the big pieces of wood that are used to hold railroad tracks together. Crossties are about 10 feet long, 12 inches wide and 8 inches thick and soaked in wood preservative called "creosote." They may weigh between 200 and 300 pounds.

In my youth when the railroad put new crossties under the railroad tracks, they simply pitched the old ones over the bank. There the honeysuckle vines, briars and locust trees covered them. The easily retrievable ones the locals took home to use to make hog lots and for fence posts. But, there were lots left for the more industrious and hardy.

In the spring of 1965 we — Terry Albert, Jimmy Bland, Gary Long, Gary Bishop and I — scoured the railroad right-of-way for old crossties. Terry and I actually did most of the scouring. If we could get Terry's old jeep near the crosstie, we'd drag it out. Hard-to-reach ties we pitched into the river and herded downriver to the future site of the "Crosstie Cabin."

Now, getting them out of the river was a job only a fool or a boy with too much time on his hands would take on. Here a strong back was most helpful. A weak mind was paramount! You simply waded out into the mud up to your waist and kind of wrestled the ties to the riverbank, then wrapped a chain around a crosstie and hooked it to the jeep. You might be covered with mud head to toe, but you quickly learned not to rub your eyes in this process or the creosote might blind you! I did this only once, and the next day it seemed like I needed two pairs of glasses.

After each trip upriver, we would build a little onto the crosstie cabin. In the beginning it wasn't hard at all. You see, it was just a one crosstie square structure, so we just picked up a crosstie and set it on top of the last one. No, it was not built like a log cabin where the corners are crossed for strength. We just laid them kind of end-to-end in a square, with no overlapping. We would have built the crosstie cabin in true log cabin style if we had ever heard of such a thing.

Everyone that looked at this structure and said, "You

sorry rascals! That thing is going to fall on you and kill you. Then look at the work you will have wasted."

Notice here that no one is too concerned about us, just our labor. Notice no suggestion for a safer building method from more knowledgeable adults. In our defense, we thought that if we were lucky enough to get the walls built "without being killed" we could make the roof out of crossties, too. By damn, it won't fall then anyway!

Day after day, the walls grew higher and the crossties became harder to find and move. By the time we were lifting them six feet, they were getting really heavy, and the walls were right wobbly. That's when Terry decided the walls were high enough, and we started placing crossties across for the roof. With the first two or three, I was afraid that each move just might be our last. But again, the luck of youth prevailed. Another thing unique to this little abode was there were no nails used. The structure stood because of the sheer weight of the crossties.

We made it, and the cabin was finished. Well almost. There was no door. It was just a great big square building. Our thinking was simple, "One thing at a time." Our plan to make a door would come after the walls and roof were up. Chuck Shorter came to our aid with a chainsaw as big as a crosstie. In just a few minutes we had a front door. It was the only opening to the entire cabin.

When I walked in, I soon realized that I could not stand

upright. I had to walk bent over. We could not build up any higher; the only other option was to go down. We dug out the floor, down about three or four feet.

Now anyone 10 feet or less could stand up. We dug it deep so Chuck could stand up, too. He is about 6'6" possibly even 7' tall. We also needed room for his cap. That is if he or anyone else could see to stand up. With no windows and no lights, it was as dark as Davie Jones' Locker was deep.

After all of the crosstie-carrying and floor-digging, we discovered that there were big holes in the roof. We took to scouting the countryside looking for boards to make a roof. We were in luck! We came across a stash of used tin. These were long and wide sheets, and their original intent was roofing, so cabbaging them off seemed just right, in a way. The tin went back to work, and we stayed somewhat dry.

Now everything was complete at last. Good strong walls, a floor deep enough to walk in and a roof that did not leak too much. It was still so dark that you needed a flashlight to get around in the daytime. But that was okay.

We added an old couch that smelled like a wet hound dog, plus a few old armchairs that we found setting next to the road headed for the trash dump. We picked up a small wooden table from storage in Uncle Shorty's barn. All of our newly found furnishings were set right down on the dirt floor. It was Home Sweet Home, except for the damp dirt floor, mold, mildew, millions of crawling bugs and all the spiders. But, what the heck, Home Sweet Home anyway. Almost overnight the cloth on the couch and chairs took on an almost white color; the mold started to grow real fast.

The only thing missing was a cook stove. As luck would have it, a very small cast iron heat stove was donated. Daddy called it a "laundry stove." Please do not ask me why; only he knows for sure. We put it in the cabin, complete with three joints of stovepipe.

When a fire was built, the cabin took on a very different smell. The mold and mildew went into hiding in the dirt walls for a while. The musty smell gave way to the smell of warm melting creosote. One made me cough, while the other just made me wheeze. But when you are 12 years old, your health ain't anything to be worried about anyway.

One late fall night it was raining, all of the wood was real wet, and the crosstie cabin was as cold as a meat locker. It was so cold a lot of the mold died, but there was a thin layer of mud on the floor. Jimmy Bland was building a fire in the stove, and I was sitting in the dark on a sofa. Time after time, Jimmy put a match under the damp paper and wet wood. The fire just was not going to catch up, so Jimmy poured three or four glugs of gas from the outboard motor gas can right into the stove. This was a metal can with a rubber hose, kept right there in the cabin. When Jimmy struck the next match, the stove lit up with a crack like thunder, the lid flew off and the door was blown open. In the cabin was a ball of fire as bright as the 4th of July that reached into every corner. The top of the gas can had also started to burn with a soft rumbling sound within.

I didn't know what to do. There was flame at least 15 inches tall right there on top of the gas-can hose. The can is between me and the door. Out of instinct or fear, I put my hand tight over the metal spout to cut off the oxygen until the fire went out. I had one badly burned hand, but I was alive. Jimmy Bland looked at me with no eyebrows and singed hair and said, "Well, that was close, but the fire is starting to catch."

We settled down like nothing had happened. The gas can was never set outside. You did not want to take a chance that rainwater would get in the gas.

Get ready for this! After a year or two, we boys were bigger and the Crosstie Cabin was getting smaller, so we had to expand. We had a bigger boat, and Terry now had a 3½ horsepower outboard motor. Our traveling range was greater than ever before. This meant we could cabbage off crossties much farther up river. The goal was to build a second story on the crosstie cabin, which we did, this time using lumber to build the roof. Still, the floor was nothing more than the old original tin roof, and this would never do for a fine abode like this one.

One day Bobby Ray stopped by. He liked what he saw, but he did not know what he was in for. Bobby Ray had a pickup truck. One night really late we loaded up and drove to a construction site just barely outside of Blacksburg. We were looking for flooring; you know, something to cover the old tin. There it was! We backed up to a stack of plywood and loaded up enough to make a fine floor. While we were at it, we got enough to sheet the interior with fresh, new ½-inch plywood.

Now this cabin was built to last. And it did for years. About every day, as I drive home I think about this. We cabbaged off the plywood from a home being built not a stone's throw from where I live today. Strange world, isn't it?

The old "Crosstie Cabin" was heavily used for 10 or 15 years, until it was destroyed by a grass fire most likely set by fishermen. From what I hear, the cabin looked like a whole town on fire. Just about the time it burned, a young lady from Virginia Tech vanished. Investigators dug through the ashes looking for her remains. Thank goodness all the investigators found were old liquor bottles, bent nails and smallish thick clumps of boy sweat. Sadly, the body of the young woman has never been found.

Me and Shorty and Old Ted

In the winter of 1973, I bought the little cinderblock house on the river from Mr. Hubert Grissom. It was always call "Grissom's Cabin," so I just never did try to change the name of it. Kind of like the "Bus" was just the bus.

As a little kid, I always thought that someday I would own it or at least a place like it. In partial payment for Mr. Grissom digging our well up on River Ridge, Uncle Shorty took Old Ted, the horse, and sledded all the cinderblock, sand and gravel down over the hill to build this old cabin. At the time, if Uncle Shorty did something, I did it too. So over a course of about three weeks, every afternoon after work we moved building materials to the site where the cabin would someday be built. Some 20 years later I moved in. Now how is that for a story? If you want, I can tell you about cleaning out the old steep road and making the first car road down over the hill. Now I have moved to the river full time. It is 100 feet outside my door.

A Watchdog that Did not Need to Bark

Along the river, things just get cabbaged off more often than when one is living along the car road, so everyone needs to have a good watchdog. Early on down at Grissom's Cabin, you could not set anything down; someone would just cabbage it off. (That is a much nicer way of saying some lowlife cretin would abscond with your possession – some would say steal it.) Not far from the cabin, there was a small building that Mr. Grissom used as a pony shed. The pony could go in the lower part and get out of the rain. In the upper part he kept a few bales of hay and a little pony grain. Damn little pony grain, I might say.

Here is an interesting aside. When Mr. Grissom was at the cabin, he would feed the pony hay. In the fall and winter, he rarely went to the river, so the pony rarely got fed. That pony went somewhat wild. He would swim the river and graze in the pines. He would eat the moss in the river. He would walk up to Cloyd Pike's and eat honeysuckles. Poor Old Trula Pike said she fattened him on cold biscuits. When he showed up at our hog lot, I would pitch him an ear of corn now and then. Sometimes he would jump over the fence at Uncle Shorty's and eat with the hogs. I always thought that was funny. We all kept a bale of hay for the wondering rascal. He liked table scraps, too. He may not have eaten very well, but he sure ate regularly, and he managed to stay alive.

I was at this point the proud owner of Grissom's Cabin. One day I put a sack of corn out in the little barn to feed the ducks, and within hours it seemed like the rats had eaten all the corn. Mice and rats came from everywhere. Some must have traveled more than five miles; they just had to. There were so many that they wore their paths real slick. I started setting traps everywhere.

Another day in the spring, I looked up on one of the rafters, and there was a big black snake. I do not know why, but I named him Fred. Not much time passed before Fred had friends. Two more snakes showed up, then three and then more than I was going to count. A big black snake hung from each rafter.

Somehow word got around about the snakes, and you could put anything in that building, and no one would touch it. I kept an outboard motor, trotlines, a lawn mower and no one touched a thing. Including the snakes, they never touched anyone at all, but that did not matter. One day my brother Mike was mowing the yard, and when he finished he started running with the mower toward the building. He got to within about 25 feet and turned the mower loose. As the mower rolled to the shed, I asked him why he did not put it in the shed like a normal person would. He said, "No one but a fool would keep a building full of snakes, and I am not going in there." No one was going to mess with Fred.

Another thing that I always found funny was that since snakes are cold-blooded, they go somewhere else during the winter. That means Fred left the building in the winter. That did not matter. The old snakeskins hanging on the ceiling rafters were enough of a reminder.

The Time I Rode a Log Downriver to Fishing Run

When I heard Daddy, Shorty, Gilbert Hilton, Mod, Nelson and any other quarter-of-the-way drunk man tell this story, he would talk about the times they would find an old log, stump or piece of a boat in the edge of the river and climb on and ride all the way from the Flannigan Farm to Fishin Run, then ride a coal train home. I think they just loved to talk about setting on their float of choice and fishing and swimming all day while slowly working their way down river. They talked about waving to people on the bank as they floated by.

My great ride took place in the late spring of 1964; I was about 12 years old. I was either in the sixth or seventh grade at Prices Fork Elementary School. The river had been high, near flood stage, for a few days. A friend and I were talking at lunch. Carl said that the river was still real high. He would have known, since he lived mostly on what Daddy called the

"Bell Farm." Sometimes he lived in the old Jonny Morris house upon Lover's Leap, too. I liked the idea that he could just live anywhere he wanted. Me, I pretty much just came and went where and when I wanted, too. But his living arrangements were different. I had to live in my parents' house.

Well anyway, he saw the river every day. I did not. He informed me that the river was going down, so the next Saturday morning I went to the river by myself to check things out. Now, this was strictly something I was forbidden to do. If I had gotten caught, I would have been threatened with an ass-busting of gigantic proportions. (A big ass-busting was almost never actually given, but the threat Mom and Elmer both liked.) I was not worried about an ass-busting. Threats they came and went. The river stayed, and it needed watching over and looking after. So I always went. Here's how I remember it.

The river is still very high, but well back within its banks. I am walking in the slick mud and grass, when I find a very nice tree trunk. It has few limbs and no stump. It is just floating, caught in the laps just above Mod Snider's little house. I simply step into the water and give it a push. The water is so cold that it wants to take my breath. I just hang on. I am moving so slow that I have to help paddle the log down the river. It truly takes forever, it seems, to get to Whitethorn. I am thinking that I'll get off there at the mouth of Tom's Creek, as soon as all of the fishermen see me.

As I get close to the mouth of the creek there is no one to wave to or holler at. I am thinking, "You need someone to see you or your ride is all for nothing." I make my mind up to go on down the river a ways. Surely there will be a fisherman to catch a ride back upriver with. Again, you need someone to tell the story for you at Tom Long's Store; it makes the story more real. You just cannot tell it yourself. I ride all the way to the lower end of the big bottom on the Bell Farm, swim to the bank and start walking back up the railroad. I do catch a train just below Whitethorn. I get off at the railroad gate and walk up the holler.

I have a real strong sense of pride in doing what I have done, but there is no good way to tell this story. For example, I walk up to Uncle Nelson's. I find him near the hog lot. He rolls me one those half-and-half cigarettes and gives me a small drink of licker while I start telling my story. All that sorry rascal has to say to me is, "It is a damn wonder you did not drown. Look at all the mud and stuff all over you. Them clothes are ruined. Money don't grow on trees."

I later told people this and they laughed at me and called me a big liar. I guess that some stories are best kept quiet about. So from here on I am not going to tell anymore about riding a log downriver. You may think it is a tall tale, but I did it.

Life's Little Lessons

I learned a good lesson muskrat trapping, one that will stick with me to the day I die. I learned it the hard way. I had set more than 30 muskrat traps from the cabin upriver, all the way to the Radford Arsenal Property. It was late in the season, and only a very few people were still trapping. All went well on Friday night when I set the traps, but by Saturday morning I had taken only one or two muskrats. There were footprints in the fresh snow, and I figured on Saturday mornings there could be a duck hunter or two, possibly someone was out for a few late season squirrels, plus early Saturday was a great time for a walk. You see, there were always good explanations for footprints in the snow.

I just did not think about poachers and thieves. Not here on New River, and not in a place like this. Sunday morning, it was easy to see some of the traps were gone. Yes, someone had stolen them. A few weeks earlier, Daddy and Shorty had given me some names of unsavory people that tended to prowl along the river just looking for mischief to get into. They were folks to keep an eye out for. Uncle Shorty warned, "They will steal the pennies off'n of a dead man's eyes. They steal just for the fun of stealing stuff." Well, I just had not been careful at all, and I paid for it.

To make things worse, in a few days I went to Tom Long's store and all of my longtime friends just looked at me kind of real funny like. I was now being accused of stealing someone else's traps. As the story went, Mr. So and So had set a line of traps from the Whiterock to Lover's Leap, and on Sunday morning most of his traps were gone and muskrats taken from some, too. My so-called friends said I was greedy and wanted all of the muskrats for myself.

I just paid for my Dr. Pepper and my hunk of cheese and walked out. I could not think of one thing to say to defend myself. There was one man in the store that never looked up at me and never spoke one word. He was on the top of Daddy and Shorty's list. Honestly, I cannot say for sure that he took them. Most likely I will never know for sure. But I very rarely went back to the store unless I just needed something and could not find it somewhere else. My association with the store and this set of people was over. Dirty Neck Wiley told me later that he did not think that I took Mr. So and So's traps, and he thought I was right to just walk away. I still remain the victim here.

To this day I have not spoken to the gentleman, but in some ways I thank him for a great lesson. Now you are asking yourself, just how does a person tell your trap from another person's traps? When you buy them, they are exactly the same. Everyone has their mark on each trap. Mine had six file marks on the spring handle, just like Elmer's. You might pick it up by accident, you might not know who it belongs to, but for damn sure you know it isn't yours. Life was great; it just wasn't always snowy moonlight nights with Kentucky Gentleman and Winston Cigarettes at your side.

Elmer and Shorty were right. In the words of Elmer, "Just know that there are people out there that would much rather steal a nickel from you than have you give them a shiny new quarter!"

A Reputation Follows You

A reputation seems to follow a person. To some, I was now a thief. Tried and convicted of stealing my own traps. Now, please keep in mind that I was no angel, and I make no claim as to ever being one. In the spring of that year, the river had been up, and lots of things had washed downriver. One morning, I found a very good-looking boat in front of the cabin. The only problem was it was stuck on a stump with a very large hole in its plywood bottom.

I knew the owner would come looking for a nice boat like this. It could be fixed in an hour or two with a new sheet of plywood. So, I drug it up on the bank and set it up on two old crossties. My plan was, if no one claimed it after a month or so, I would fix it and use it. The boat stayed there for a month or more, and one morning I got a knock on the cabin door. The boat owner and a friend of mine were standing there. The boat owner looked real mad and said, "This man here said you have my boat. This man saw my boat in your yard." I asked both men to come into the cabin and told them that there was a boat setting down by the water's edge with a hole in it.

I was not thanked for finding it and holding onto it for him. I was right out accused of stealing it. I told this man that the boat had washed up here a month or so ago and that the hole in the bottom was from a stump near my boat landing. I showed him the stump. I also asked if he had the key to the boat's lock or proof that he really was the owner. The lock that had held the boat to its mooring was still on it, and his key unlocked it. I asked the question, "If I had stolen your boat, doesn't it make sense that I would have taken the lock off the chain and not gone to the trouble of knocking a hole in the bottom and laying the boat up here so the owner could find it?"

I got no answer! Both men could remember the high water, and it coincided with the loss of the boat. I asked the man to load his boat and leave. This friend of mine came back later and said to me, "I am sorry that I did not ask you about the boat first. The boat owner knows that you did not steal the boat; the high water even broke the black willow it was tied to." I never spoke to my so-called friend again to the day he died. Yes, it is true: no good deed ever goes unpunished.

Daddy and Shorty never locked their boats, and neither did I. Shorty always said, "The best way to lose a boat is to lock it. Keep it unlocked and tell people where the paddle is hidden in the weeds, and it will always be there when you need it." Well, most of the time it will be there.

People asked me why I would let snakes live in the little building by my cabin. My only answer was a question: "How did you know there were snakes in there?" Well, I kept them there to skeer off people just wanting to steal something.

Now what do I want you to learn from this story? First, never play in the frozen river the way I did. You just might not be as lucky as me. I hear freezing to death is no fun. Also, thieves are out there! And if a thief is low down enough to steal muskrat traps, by damn he will steal anything. Be a little suspicious of tracks in the snow. If they look like wolf tracks, most likely that is what they are, and don't rationalize them into chicken tracks like I did. Now that is a fool's folly. They are wolves, and you need to stay the hell away from them. I also learned to keep my mouth shut about what I was up to. The fewer people that know what you are up to, the better.

Most of all, I learned the meaning of fair-weather friend and real honest-to-goodness friend. If I caught Chuck Shorter, Terry Albert or Jimmy Bland in my house at night with the light off, I knew that they needed something and out of respect they did not want to cut the light on or wake me up. There is no need to question more! Just go on back to sleep, or get on up and give them a hand. There are others that, if you catch them in your house, you had better damn well shoot first, possibly shoot two times, then ask questions. Them there sons-of-a-bitches want to kill you and rob you blind.

Paddling the Canoe Through the Cabin Door

I had been living in the cabin a year or so at the time of this story, so it must have been about the winter of 1974 - 1975. Now, it had been raining for at least a week, and the river had been coming up steadily. I was not awfully worried. The water had gotten within three feet of the cabin two times before, but the river had never risen into the cabin. Still, people were telling me that this was going to be the flood of the century. Not since the 20s had it flooded like this.

After all, the water did come into the cabin, but it was not more than a foot deep and took only a few days to dissipate. The entire cabin needed a very good mopping, and the black and red shag carpet had to go. Truth is, it had needed throwing away when it was given to me.

The high water also washed away my winter's supply of firewood. Now that was a truly a big loss. I got to thinking that now that the flood of the century was over, I could set back and never have to worry about flooding again in my lifetime. By the end of the month, all of the trash had been picked up and pitched back into the river, and I'd been cutting firewood almost every day. It had been very cold, and the ground was frozen solid two or three inches. When it warmed up a little, enough snow fell to cover the ground six to ten inches. All of a sudden, the weather chose to warm up into the 40s and 50s, and rain started to fall. The snow melted quickly, leaving nowhere for the water to go, except downriver. The river started up fast. Mod Snider and I went to the cabin and removed everything that we could, just in case it chose to flood again. The rest of my stuff we stacked up on the bar in the center.

I was now sitting at the car bridge at Whitethorn, just watching the water rise up and up some more. David and Pat Price joined me in the watching. Woolf drove up, too, in his old '49 Chevrolet pickup he bought from Owen Summers. We watched the water cross the road to the bridge. I said, "Well, I think it is about three feet from the door."

I had just seen it this high less than six weeks before. Within an hour, we figured that water would be in the cabin and coming up the walls. So we drove to the cabin and discovered that our math was wrong. The water was way up the wall much higher than we ever expected. It was probably as much as four feet deep in the cabin.

One of the last things I had done, that morning, before I moved out, was tie a rope to the big homemade picnic table and secure it to a water fountain in the yard. When we got to the cabin, the table was floating high and lunging like a horse on a rope. After seeing the table and some careful thinking, we decided that the best thing to do was open the cabin door and all of the windows so that the water could flow through. David said that would reduce the pressure on the walls. I truly was in favor of this. You see, they had not invented flood insurance back then. Even if they had, I most likely could not have afforded it anyway.

The only way to open the door and let the angry water have a way out was to pull one of the canoes from out of the weeds on the railroad right-of-way into the floodwater. This was not the smartest thing I have ever done. I have never been known to let lack of intelligence get in the way of a good plan. I paddled to the cabin, reached down to the door lock and pushed open the front door. It is truly an eerie feeling to paddle into a flooded house. I guess it worked. The cabin was still standing the next morning and the day after, too.

The clean-up this time was a community effort. There was river mud thick on the floor. You could not walk inside the cabin without sinking in the mud. Melanie Ottin, Toby Tomlin, Chuck and Joan came with shovels to clear the first layer from the floor. The walls had a mud line five feet up the side. Everything in the building was destroyed. It was a mess. After it was cleaned up and dried out, people just started cleaning out their basements and bringing me new (used) furniture. I now had a somewhat newer bed, and two orange Naugahyde sofas. Then there was a red sofa, too, and countless mismatched dishes.

Life moves on, and two once-in-a-century floods had occurred just six weeks apart. I guess one must have happened the last day of the past century and the second on the first day of the new century. She is a beauty, that Old New River, but you had better keep one eye on her. Uncle Shorty was right!

My First Canoe

I wish that I could do my canoeing all over again; I cannot. For now, it is enough to know that I had the time and the chance that so many never had. There is just something about the New River, a canoe, and a half-raised, red-neck boy with not one care in the world.

When I was a teen and young adult, Uncle Nelson would say to people that I was the "last of the wild men." I often wondered about this statement. I must have been a sight rougher than I thought I was. Probably he meant that I was rather single-minded when it came to the river. I never thought about myself as anything other than a regular old run-of-the-mill boy. When I was in my heyday with that old black and white fiberglass canoe, I had enough wild experiences to fill two lifetimes. I had more fun than a puppy with two peters.

The year was 1970. I was working at the Mick or Mack

Grocery Store in Blacksburg and talking with one of the bread deliverymen. Up to this point in my life, I had never ridden in a canoe or even wanted one. Only wooden flat-bottom johnboats were used on the New River. I had seen a canoe one time at Boy Scout Camp, but I never got to ride in one. In fact, I'd never seen anyone ride in the things. I wish that I had; it might have been right helpful later on.

Anyway, the Merita Bread man asked me if it was true that I lived in a little house along New River, just upriver from Whitethorn. He said that he and his father had passed the house a few weekends ago. He went on to tell me that their canoe had turned over near Eggleston, they lost everything and almost drowned. He asked me if I'd ever wanted a canoe or knew of anyone that might have an interest in one. He very much wanted to sell or get rid of the canoe he and his dad now considered a deathtrap. In fact, he was ready to sell the canoe, two paddles and two lifejackets for $100 dollars. All that had cost him more than $500. Yes, back in the day, 1970 that is, things were much cheaper.

On Saturday, I drove to Dublin to look at the canoe, and the very minute I saw it I knew that the Huckleberry Finn in me wanted it just to be free. I said "Sold" before the bread man even quoted me a final price. I never even asked if he would take less than $100. That old Obsessive Compulsive Disorder grabbed me and would not turn me loose. Heck, I still battle OCD to this day. I will tell you about that some other time; right now I am canoeing.

I loaded the thing up and drove right to Terry Albert's house. We went straight to Whitethorn and put the canoe in the river. The wind was blowing so hard that no one in their right mind would go out on the river in a johnboat, much less a canoe. It was early March, the water was cold enough to make your heart just stop beating with hypothermia, and the air temperature was no more than 45 degrees. There were little white-capped waves more than a foot high. We put the canoe in the water, and it almost blew away before I could get in. I grabbed a paddle, stepped right in, and came very close to landing on my head there at the boat landing. If Terry had not grabbed the side, I might have been going to the hospital, not for a canoe ride.

I was now in the canoe, setting on the front seat, pointing toward the back seat. I thought this was the correct way to paddle. Terry jumped in and was forced to set backwards on the front seat – yes, the little one. We were both setting ass-backwards, facing one another. I had never seen a canoe paddled. The sad thing is I did not know the difference. I should tell you that Terry is pretty smart, too. He might have known the difference, but was afraid that I might want to shift seats. This could have been a death wish in this water. This was no time for anything but getting back to the boat landing alive.

Terry might have been trying not to hurt my feelings. No, that cannot be the reason. My feelings had never mattered before. We were too busy paddling backwards and dipping water. Did I tell you that it was early March and colder than all get out? When we did get to the boat landing, I was happier than a pig in slop to be on land and to be the owner of a backwards canoe. Terry looked like he had been slopping hogs, and he was cold. I ran the truck heater all the way to his house, talking 90 miles an hour about all that we could do this summer.

Well, Jimmy Bland said that he had ridden in a canoe before, maybe at Boy Scout Camp or somewhere. He might even have seen it done on television. Jimmy was much worldlier than me. He even lived in Blacksburg. I trusted in his wisdom. Jimmy was always easy to talk to, and he understood the situation.

We were paddling around one day, and Jimmy said, "Just sit still for a damn second, you hard-headed butt; just set still and shut up." (Only he did not say butt, and he used a right stern voice on me, too.) So I did, and he just turned around in the back seat and pointed the canoe in the right direction and started paddling. Now he said, "You, hard-headed rascal, if you think you can turn on your seat, do so." I turned around, and Jimmy said, "Now just sit there and see how much better the correct way is to ride." The next time Jimmy let me drive some. He was right. Try to trust me on this — after a while I became very good at canoe paddling.

Now I had lived my whole life up on River Ridge, but I had never ventured downriver any farther than the riffle at Bell Springs. So one day, Jimmy and I took a trip that would carry us all the way to Daddy Jim Price's Farm in Pembroke. Man, the river was smooth as a piece of glass. When I was about

8 years old, Daddy had made me stop picking up potatoes to look at a flock of 15 geese going over. "You may never see geese like this again." Now, ten years later, just above Bell Springs, in the long shallow flat water sat a flock of geese; there must have been 25 or 30 of them. When they took off, they flew up the Fishing Run side of the river. The sun was low and in my eyes. It was something to see. The geese flew against a backdrop of trees. The best part was the reflection of the trees and the geese that just moved effortlessly right up the river. I have never forgotten this scene. It needed to be made into a post card or a picture for a calendar. The scenery only got better.

In the little community of Eggleston the big cliffs came all the way to the river, and there was a very deep fishing hole. According to the old stories, the Whorl Hole is much deeper than the Whiterock Hole. Oh, deeper by far. Shorty and Mod warned me to stay away from the Whorl Hole. "You can get yourself sucked down right to the bottom and never come up. It is the truth if I am standing here," they said. Again, according to the Official Old Story Record, (The OOSR is an unwritten record truly never seen by anyone, but all old men know about it and swear by its indisputable accuracy.) everything from old-timey steam trains to modern coal trains has fallen in the Whorl Hole and vanished. Hundreds upon hundreds of people have seen it happen; some have even lost their lives trying to get a better look.

Jimmy and I could not find it. We paddled all over the place looking for it. Surely there would be a pile of old undigested train engines on the bank or something marking the place. But there were no markers. For all I know, the Whorl Hole might have eaten a train in the last day or two, and because of that wasn't interested in us or something.

Chuck and I took the same ride some time later. We packed up a good lunch, took a case of Blue Ribbon beer and started off. We did not want the beer to get too warm, so we hooked the cans on a fish stringer and let them trail behind us in the river. When we got near to Mr. Price's, there was a big set of riffles. Most of the Blue Ribbon cans were now rolling around in the canoe. Few, very few, were still on the stringer. As we got closer to the riffles, I took a piece of rope and tied my leg to the canoe.

Chuck said, "You are crazy."

I answered, "Where this thing goes I am going, too." Many of the Blue Ribbons must still have been rolling around in me. This may have been an omen for future stories.

The truth is I did like that canoe, and where it went I wanted to go! It was the key to all river-riding. Only on very rare occasions did you even see another canoe. A young man who lived up the road from me and I were about the only ones who even had canoes. Today, 30 years later, there are three canoe services in Giles County alone that will take you on this trip. Poor old New River is looked at more than ever!

Well, anyway, she is a pretty ride! If you are in the mind

to question me on this, set in a canoe just about the islands on an early fall evening about two hours before dark. Look upriver, then downriver. The scenery makes it so hard to decide which way is the right way to go. Only after I left the river for good did I fully understand that sitting in a canoe makes a grand experience even better. No, I cannot go back; I am just glad that I went.

White Water, White Knuckles

Not everything was a pretty ride. Sometimes my canoe decisions were about as dumb as anything one could imagine. For example, one summer when I was about 20 years old and still right impressionable, it had rained for two solid weeks or more. The river was at flood stage, and some of the smaller streams that on most days were no more than a foot deep were now raging forces.

"So what are we going to do today?" asked a neighbor from up the road. "We need to head up to Poverty Creek just to see how fast the water is moving. I bet the Kittle Rock is something to see."

He was wrong. It was not fast-moving; it was at least a Class 5 rapid, might have been a Class 6 if the scale went that high. We looked back and forth at one another. Holy Macaroni! No way was I getting any closer than where I stood. The roar of the falls was so loud that you had to holler to be heard. I cannot find words to tell you how dangerous this water was. Boulders that were usually up on the bank were sticking out of the water; trees were submerged in the water; and brush and debris were rushing past. You could even hear large rocks beating together as they moved under the force of the water.

As I write this, I am still thinking that I am lucky to be here. We looked for something less dangerous. We went up near the bridge over Tom's Creek, the one just below Nutter's Store. The water was out in the big field. We unloaded the canoes on the hardtop road and paddled out the car road toward the car bridge. Tom's Creek was full of brush, the banks were covered with tree limbs and the water was moving very fast. Before you could turn around, we were passing the spot where Poverty Creek dumps into Tom's Creek. In one paddle stroke the creek was twice as big as before. It was meaner by a factor of four.

Truly, I was fighting for my life trying to get to the shore about 10 feet away. It was impossible to get there because of the current and the trees. Downstream, you could hear the water crashing against the cliff behind Old Edgar Mason's house. This was getting really serious. In just one blink of an eye, I entered Mason's property, and there was a small break between the trees in the turn before the cliff. We made it! The water was crashing into the cliff and raising water 20 feet up the cliff face. Truly I thought that we were very, very lucky to get out of this adventure with our lives.

Two days later, when the floodwaters had passed, I went back to Edgar Mason's. The normal flow of water was being forced up the cliff face about six inches, and the creek was no more than four or five feet across. The rush of water was making almost no sound at all. You may be saying to yourself that an experience like this would make a person smarter. Well, for you it might, but it just made me happy to be alive and breathing and with little thought of tomorrow. It takes a lot more to make me, a true Appalachian American Red-neck Boy, smarter. But, I can promise you, an expanded intelligence and understanding are coming!

This next canoe ride that happened may be even more stupid. Almost the same flooding situation happened the next year. This time, we were going to tackle Strouble's Creek. Yes, Strouble's is the little spring branch that runs under the Virginia Tech drill field. It fills the duck pond and slowly makes its way to the river. On a hot day in the summer it offers no more challenge than two good-sized garden hoses.

A group of close friends talked me into this trip. I have a weak memory, don't I? I must have forgotten the ride to Edgar Mason's. I cannot remember who all took part in this fool's folly, but a close friend was in the canoe with me, and I am very happy that he was. I have always thought that I owed him something for his effort. I am not joking here one bit. Possibly I owe him my life!

We started down a stream that on a regular day was no more than two feet wide and possibly three to six inches deep

— not even big enough to float a canoe. This day, Strouble's Creek was a good ten feet wide and six feet deep and running in full flood stage way out into the brush and weeds in the banks. It was dangerous to even be standing on the car bridge, and that is just pure fact.

That alone should have made a normal man say, "No." The operative word here is normal; I ain't been called that too often. I must have been 21 to 22 years old. The first canoe was helped into the creek, and the thing vanished in a flash. The second canoe took off, and then it was time for us. Within a second, it was taking every piece of skill I had to keep the canoe upright and dodge the overhanging limbs, thick brush, large floating logs, wire fences and roots. Now I have to admit, this was fun! Fat boys like to do this kind of stuff; they do. Possibly, the group was right: "We just need to do this so we can say we did." We ducked under barbed-wire fences, somehow dodged fallen trees avoiding decapitation and passed the pieces of old water racks leaving nothing but a cable across the creek.

All of a sudden, we approached a single strand of barbed-wire fence no more than one foot above the water. Now, keep in mind we were moving at the speed of floodwaters. There was nowhere to go. No one but a fool or an escapee from Saint Alban's Mental Hospital, over in Radford, would have even been near here. But yet here I was, and I ain't ever been to Saint Albans yet!

We ducked as low in the canoe as we could. The wire was sliding down the gunnels. It caught my lifejacket and pulled me from the canoe. I was held by the wire. I was not strong enough to pull myself upstream against the current to untangle myself. About every five seconds, I was pulled underwater for a second or two. This was getting pretty serious and real annoying, when all of sudden something hit me hard enough to break my ribs. It was my canoeing partner. Somehow he had gotten to the bank and had come back for me. He took a paddle and chopped me off the wire, and I floated downstream to an open space.

I could have kissed him, but the rest of the group would have looked at me funny. While all of this was happening to me, one of the party had been caught in a small hydraulic. These were created by one of the many newly formed low head dams. His canoe had been destroyed. The whole side was taken off. He was lucky that he wasn't drowned. I guess we would have had to tie him to a canoe or dragged out his dead self like a dead deer. Fortunately, we did not have to do this. I truly wanted to get out of there. I had finally learned that my floodriding days were about over.

Now, I am not the sharpest tool in the shed, no sir, far from it. But, I have wised up a lot through these two experiences. When I tell people this they laugh and say, "What a lie!" But I ask you not to do what I have done.

There are many other little stories that I could share, but at the moment it just seems like I have forgotten most of them. You see, I once had a black-and-white striped canoe, a green one and George Shorter's yellow aluminum one. Each had its own way of leading me to different adventures. I learned to lay trotlines from a canoe. I also gigged from a canoe. I would paddle up to the rock bar and let the canoe drift at will down river towards the islands. I would kill a fish now and then, but I was no gigger. I guess I am to be a boat poler forever. But, I still remember canoe trips. I am now older, and there are more people on poor old New River than ever. I saw a 100-horsepower jet boat a few weeks ago from my seat in my old canoe. I still paddle. Guess I just do not know how to do it any other way.

Rock Diving

Yesterday, I went fishing down at the old bus. It was quiet except for the non-stop hum of the Radford Arsenal and the passing of an occasional motorboat. Now, of course, the old bus isn't there anymore. Long ago, Kevin chopped it up and sawed it up, then pushed it over the riverbank. But the name is still there, and really that is all that is important anyway. All you got to say is, "I am going down to the bus," and everyone for miles around knows where you are headed. I walked past the picnic shelter that Luke, Kyle and Kevin have built on the path to Whiterock. The shelter backs up to the historical path walked by our parents and grandparents to the river. Years ago this whole place all looked bigger somehow. On my little walk, I saw lots of fish jumping and swimming near the shore.

There were very big carp, many smallmouth bass and several redeyes, none of which wanted to get themselves caught. So, I kept walking. When I got to the rock I just cast my craw-

111

fish and reflected back on how many times in the past I had sat in this very same spot, 100, 500, possibly 1,000 times. Only someone with a better counter than me can know the exact number for sure. But, I can remember setting on this tree root looking out toward the big ledge watching my brothers and sisters master the fine art of rock diving. I remember a whole list of funny stories about this spot.

Rock diving is something practiced only by the most capable red-neck boys and girls. It is not for the faint of heart, either. For sure, it is no place for a town boy. Since it was practiced only in the summer months, you had all winter to plan and work out better training systems. To start with, you needed a rock about the size of your head, or a little bigger in my case. You see, I was little more rotund than the average red-necked boy. The rock's role, in all this, was to push you down deep into the river quickly. This would give you some time to look at things on the way back up.

Now, here is how we did it. I am sure there were many other ways, but this was ours. First off, you found up your old folding chairs and a cooler. Some put cold beer in the cooler, while others added in a Double Cola or two, because they were big. Next, you and your friends went out to a shallow ledge. For rock diving, it is best to have a sharp-edged ledge with a smooth face. It is also nice to have a straight drop off -- say, 20 feet or more. (We were in luck. Right beside the bus was the Whiterock Hole.) You then found yourself a few good diving rocks. You see, it was a one-way trip for the rock into the depths of the river, so you needed at least seven or eight good rocks. It was best if you piled them up right beside your chair. You might even choose to put one in your chair to keep it from washing away. Even 50 years later, every once in awhile, a summer fishermen still cranks up a lost lounge chair.

If you were to ask any of the adults around, they would tell you the Whiterock Hole was far more than 100 feet deep. For some old-timers, it went all the way to China, with not one detour. It is not that deep now! But, back in the day, according to old-timers, whole trains went in. There were never any survivors, so there is no reason to even ask around. The whirling action of the hole sucked them down, and I mean quick! Others will tell you that if you got caught in the suck hole, your clothes would be torn off and your corpse would come up in the still waters near the community of Parrott. This is downriver about five or six miles. You see, there is a big underwater cave connecting the Whiterock Hole and Parrott. "It's got to be, just got to be." Why else would the old-timers tell you this?

In my day, I measured its depth with a piece of nylon cord and a cinder block tied on the end. In the beginning, I thought that I would need the extra weight to offset the massive current of the deep whorl hole. When I dropped the cinder block off the end of the johnboat, I thought that it might go most of the way to China. I was truly shocked when it came to rest on the bottom at a mere 26 feet. It was and still is truly a great deep hole in the river, but I do not think that it could have swallowed up a whole train as Shorty, Daddy, and Nelson had insisted. It's true, I guess, that another answer to this discrepancy could be that through the years the hole had filled up with trains, boats, skeletons, and things like that, and that means you need to be damn careful that you don't get thrown on that pile.

Everyone has a story about the Whiterock Hole. I am setting on one of the carbide cans at Tom Long's Store one night, and a bunch of old men are talking about fishing. Like always, the more they talk the bigger the fish get. Even a young, relatively unskilled fish liar, like me, can see the difference between the fish stories and lies being told. One man has just told a great story about a catfish he caught in the Whiterock Hole. It was a true river monster; it took two grown men just to get it to the bank. Everyone just listens patiently and then laughs. Well, when the laughter dies down a bit, Pride Arrington takes the floor.

All eyes turn toward him. Pride launches into this story by saying that a few days back he, too, had been fishing up at the Whiterock Hole and got his fishing line hung; well, he thought it was hung. He pulled and pulled on it. Just about the time he was fixing to cut the line, it gave a little and very slowly came loose. It was very hard to crank it up. "I thought I must have one of the biggest mud cats ever was on this line," he said.

"To my surprise," says Pride, "it weren't no catfish at all. It was one of the running lights off of Old Virginian Engine Number 3, which had been swallowed up by the Whiterock Hole a few years earlier. The most amazing thing was, the light's wick was still a-burning."

Everyone in the store breaks into a big laugh, me too. One man, the one that had caught the big mud cat a few minutes earlier, stops laughing and looks over at Pride and says, "That is a damn lie."

Pride says back to him, "Knock off 10 or 15 pounds from the big mud cat you just caught, and I will blow out that wick."

Now the whole store shakes with laughter a second time. I don't think that town people ever got to see or hear things like this.

Uncle Lake liked to tell me about how they would drop dynamite into the scary deep Whiterock Hole. He called this "fish-hunting." He said that at one time the Lytton family would put up one large barrel and three or four earthen crocks of salt fish for winter. To do this, you had to catch up the fish all at one time. At least three flat-bottom boats were required.

The first step was to tie a stick of dynamite onto a large rock -- one that would pull the dynamite straight down into the deepest part of the hole. Second, you would hook an electrical wire to the rock and the dynamite. Third, once the rock was firmly setting on the bottom, you attached the lead wire to a car battery, and the dynamite would explode. Soon after you did this, you started paddling downriver to pick up fish. Lake said that sometimes the fish came up by the time they reached the islands. Sometimes they did not come up until you were near Whitethorn. You needed to be fast, since everyone else wanted the fish, too, and people would steal them. The brothers said that fish from the size of a minnow all the way up to ones that weighed 20 to 30 pounds came up. There would be bass, catfish, pike and perch. Everything went into the salt except the pike. They got eaten fresh.

The old men at Tom Long's Store were pretty much in agreement on this next little ditty. Again, please keep mind that this is secondhand, some as much as thirdhand, information. This is not a proven fact at all. According to old-timers, once upon a time there was a limestone cavern in the bottom of the Whiterock Hole. Dynamited fish would not come up until you were way downriver. You just believe what you want of this. Even back then, I thought you had to pick through the stories to find the real true information, or even small shreds of truth, if there was any. And as the years passed and with so much dynamite-fishing, the entrance to the limestone cavern was blasted shut, I reckon.

It seems like I got off the subject of rock diving, but background information is always important and adds to your understanding of the true danger and adventure. You had to keep this stuff in mind when you started to set your chair on the rock ledges. Heck, you might be getting ready to jump into the abyss while holding onto a rock. That old river just might be in the mood to chew up and swaller a feller whole.

Once you had all of your stuff gathered up, you just

paddled the boat over to the ledge. It was not more than 50 feet from the bank. You set up your chair, piled up your rocks, and enjoyed your drink of choice. You always had to put a few rocks on your cooler so it would not float away.

How do you do the rock diving? Well, you take a good deep breath or two, pick up the rock of your choice and jump off the ledge. You go down as far as you wish. Rarely did anyone choose to go more that about 18 to 20 feet. Your head might just crack open if you went any deeper. Somewhere around this mark you turn loose of your rock, and you start up. It never takes no more than 10 to 15 seconds to swim back to the surface. It is neat looking at rock ledges. At 15 feet it is not dark by any means, but it is much darker than the surface and watching the sun change from a ruddy orange color into a brightly lit sun, now that is something.

You could do no more than a few dives with the rocks collected in one trip. You ran out of rocks very quickly, you see, and you had to paddle the johnboat across the river and get some more. On one of my dives I did see a fish, just one. I think jumping off the ledge scared the hell out of them, and he was too scared to move or something. He might have even been sick. Sometimes I was sick from visiting the cooler too much. Those Double Colas will do you in.

The Big Tree In the River

In the summer of 1965, it had rained off and on for weeks. You could see all kinds of trash, tree limbs and driftwood going down the river. Every once in a while you would see a whole treetop, limbs and roots go past. I was truly amazed by this. After the rain stopped and the river went down, I was on the river again and I found a very large tree hung on the ledges in front of the boat landing at The Whiterock. You could anchor the boat about 75 feet from it and fish. I was in need of more fishhooks and tackle, so one morning I walked to Blacksburg. There was a man working at the Blacksburg Hardware Store who knew me from when he drove a laundry truck. When he told me of a new fishing plug they had called a "Blabber Mouth Troublemaker," I bought one. It was real ugly, but I liked the name. Elmer said that it would never work, because it made too much noise. I told him it was supposed to.

Well, anyway, I could anchor near the tree and cast that

plug as close as possible, let it float a second or two, then give it a little jerk, and if there was a fish in the country it would grab hold. I know that I caught more bass and redeyes there by that tree than anywhere else I ever fished. I looked downriver past Whitethorn all the way to Parrott. If you knew what to look for, you could see the big farm at Whitethorn, too. It was just one of the prettiest places in the world. You could even see gentle summer rains coming up the river. The fish and me both liked them warm rains.

I could also see people paddling boats around Whitethorn working back and forth across the New River. They did not come above the islands much. I would go down to the riffles and pile in rocks to the point where there were no easy ways to get through with a motor. This was one of my ways of protecting my fishing territory and the fishing upriver. I guess I thought they were all mine.

It was also my tree, I thought, so I had to take care of it. I did not want others to find out just how many fish liked the tree. When I would hear an outboard boat coming, I would jump in my boat, paddle to the tree, use the boat as a diving board and generally make all kinds of racket. Fishermen just went on. I guess they thought that I was a whole lot crazy, but I kept my fish from getting caught.

Then one day, I went to the river, and my tree was gone. It just broke loose and started downriver. You could look toward the farm at Whitethorn and see it hung on a shallow rock bar, by the old barrel, near the Hubert Grissom Cabin. It stayed there for a few weeks. The next time the water came up a little, it was gone period. It was a good tree, and I hated to see it go. At Tom Long's Store, the old men just kind of looked at me. I bet they had told each other about my jumping and yelling on that tree. Well, that was ok. I did the fishing, and they just did the watching and talking.

Oh, Just to Sit on the Whiterock

One of the prettiest things I ever saw was the river covered in fog. Sometimes it would be so thick that small drops of water would stick to my eyelashes, and I would have to wipe them off.

One day I had made up my mind to go fishing, and I left the house a little before daylight. Mom always got a really happy and peaceful look all over when she sensed that I would not be coming back until suppertime or after dark. She was funny like that. Well, anyway, I made my way down through the holler in the clear early morning pre-dawn. Stars were still pretty bright. I walked over to the cliff, below the barn, just to survey things. I could not see a thing. There was a fog on the river thick enough to write your name in it. I walked on down and crossed the railroad tracks, but rather than go to the boat landing, I walked up on the Whiterock and sat down. I could hear big bass and other fish jumping and flopping, ducks and other birds waking up and flying by and other sounds of the river. I just could not see them.

About the time the sun came up, a little breeze came up with it. Within a few minutes I started to see the tops of trees along the riverbank sticking out of the fog. They were much greener than usual with the sun's first light on them. Just above the river, fog hung on tight, kind of like it was in a battle with the sun. The bright sunlight bathed me and everything above the fog. In this transition, for a minute or two, I could see the fog line up and down the river all the way to the farm at Whitethorne. In a few minutes the fog was gone, and the day got itself started, just like it had for eons. But this was the first time I had ever taken an active part. I went on fishing, but I have never forgotten just how pretty New River can be in the morning.

Grandmother always said, "When the sun burns off the fog early, it is going to be a hot, clear day." I have sat on the Whiterock many times and for many hours. It was a great place to watch dark come and light purples on the hills come crawling in, too. I always thought the stars were very clear and pretty from there.

This is also a great place to find a fox turd just chock full of small bones and fur for a younger cousin to take to school for show and tell. Not everybody has even seen a real wild fox turd. It was Thanksgiving, 2004, I think. After lunch we always walked down to the Whiterock. When I told Miss Elizabeth what I had found, her little six-year-old face just lit up with a real big smile and a twinkle in her eyes. The turd was quite a find, but nothing like watching daytime come into the world fresh and new; except maybe for Elizabeth's smile. Poor Little Elizabeth carried her prize home in her sock so she wouldn't break it; but her mother, Mary Ellen, threw the fox turd over the back fence. What a waste! Not many ever find a real honest-to-goodness wild fox turd, ever.

The Day I Left the River

Now, I do not know if this part needs a dark heading of its own, or not. You see, my heart has never truly left. My body left two times. How about "My First Trip Away From Her" for a title? But I can truly remember the last days I lived in the little cinder block cabin on the river. Yes, I can.

Well, one particular morning, I was leaving, draining the water lines and locking the door on Grissom's Cabin. I may have owned the cabin, but for some reason I could not change its name to Charles' Cabin. This day it honestly felt like it was mine, I owned her — bought and paid for — and here I was leaving.

I had an old fly rod given to me by Junior Nester. He had found it while he was working on the Virginia Tech Campus. It was my very first fly rod, and it, too, was going into the attic tomorrow morning. Real early this morning, I just walked into

124

the river and out to the rock bar in front, out past where the old barrel used to mark how high the river was. It was like I was saying good-bye to a very good friend or something. I had known nothing but this river for my whole life, and it was a very important part of that life. In many ways, my world was about 10 miles long and no more than a mile wide.

I slowly worked my way downriver. Just below the little island, there is small riffle. I cast my little red and white popping bug into the fast water. It had not drifted more than 20 feet,when one of the biggest pumpkin-seed perch I ever saw took it. I slowly worked my way down past the Big Island. In the course of the day I turned up the river on the Powder Plant side. I waded and fished to the rock bars and shallow ledges above the Tommy Bottom almost to Lovers Leap. I fished all day long. I never even took the time to eat or have a drink of water. I didn't want them, either; seemed like there was something much more important going on. My body's needs were met with clear river water, warm August sun, warm breezes and very cool shade. Fall was off somewhere, but not visible on the river yet.

It was in late August, the early morning fogs were at their peak of thickness. While the last of the early harvest apples along the river had all been eaten; the air was still very warm and the water was comfortably cool on my legs and clear as crystal. Only the occasional breeze made ripples on the water. The river had already taken on that clear early fall phase. I could see rocks deep in the water. I could see the snails hanging on them. I could see fish and lots of them. All day long, I would move close to the riffles and drop the popping bug just above the fast water, and as the lure drifted into the small eddies I would catch little small-mouth bass.

I was thinking, "Why in the world am I moving away from the river and truly the only life I have ever known."

This was one of the best days of my life. No people on the river, not one, just me. I think God must have wanted it this way. The sky was as blue as indigo, and there were lots of fish to catch. Deer even came to the water's edge and looked at me as if to say good-bye. I had not one care in the world. As dusk just started, I put the fly rod in my mouth and swam across the river to the bus and walked down the narrow dusty road to my little cinder block cabin for the last time. No, I was not going off to die; I was moving. But, I think that this day in some ways did have something in common with going off to die.

Off to the State of Rhode Island I had said that I would go. The next morning I went. As I left, I saw that the grass needed mowing. I had not chained up the canoes. All I could think of was something that I once had read by Thomas Wolfe, and how he'd said that you could never go home again. As I drove up over the railroad tracks and surveyed the river, I understood what he meant. Well, I thought that I did, anyway. I possibly could come back to the cabin and even live there, but I could never come back to the feelings of this time and place. I was about to interject new things, new people and places into my understanding. Time has a way of changing things, doesn't it? Well, I know that this must have some negative psychological implications for me. Just look at what it has done to me already. I am scared to think about tomorrow or even next week, for that matter. I do not think that I have ever been exactly right since.

I just loved living in that little cider block cabin along New River and the carefree life style that I had grown accustomed to. Wild things just need to be wild. At this moment I felt a little caged. Maybe I just might be the last of the true wild men. Sometimes I ate from the gardens, sometimes from the apple trees; sometimes I ate good fried fish, sometimes it seemed like I lived on nothing but wild greens. I got to where I could make real good fish soup, too. Once in a while, I would dine on venison, when a slow deer came by. You see, I am not a very good shot; the deer had to help me out a little.

Not since then have I paddled the boat to Lover's Leap, stripped off buck naked, turned the boat loose and just floated back to the cabin in the middle of the night with nothing but the train engines breaking the quiet. The cabin and the river were about as important in my young adult life as the bus had been in teen years. Nothing could be said but, "Good-bye, old friend."

THE COOL SIDE OF THE PILLOW

TRAPPING
GIGGING
SKINNING
CRITTERS

Putting Myself Through Junior High School

Another great thing about Tom's Creek was muskrat trapping. I like to think that I put myself through the winters of the 6th and 7th grade by muskrat trapping. On the first day of trapping season almost every boy and man went about the business of setting out a muskrat trap line. Muskrats tore up the creek bank and increased the propensity to erosion. I was still making only 75 cents an hour working, and good prime hides were worth possibly $1.50. They were the thick ones with a full winter coat. I did not catch many of them. What I caught were the early ones. Their pelts were thinner and usually brought somewhere between 75 cents and $1.00.

Actually, the value of the muskrats could be measured in two ways. One value was the amount of money they sold for. The other value was in their bragging rights. Simply put, "I caught more than you." For me the bragging rights were as important as the money! It was proof positive of your skills and your knowledge, for sure, but it also was a kind of measure of the wildness in you. It is the stuff you were made of. Stuff has yet to be defined in this case, but it was still very, very important, this stuff.

So, in late fall on the first Saturday of trapping season, I set out my 24 muskrat traps on both sides of Tom's Creek. I moved back and forth across the creek, walking on homemade stilts, setting my traps.

Mom was funny. She got up long before I did. Every morning, before daylight, she would start yelling for me to get out of bed. I would literally jump right straight up and fall into my clothes and be off. Well, that isn't all of the way true. It took about four or five good, loud hollers. I would somehow find the energy to set up on the bed and get my clothes on and walk outside. The fresh cold morning air would jolt me to fully awake before I set off in kind of a high lope, like a horse heading for the lane leading for home. Me? I was headed to the creek. I had traps to check. I doubt Huckleberry Finn or any of the Mountain Men out west took off any better than me, once they were awake that is. Now, I was fat then, too, but I could run really fast and had the wind for long runs.

I'd grab up my stilts and start checking and resetting my traps. This was always done by flashlight, and you needed to be fast. You could look up the creek and downstream and see a flashlight or two. Others were doing the same. See, you had to get done before breakfast and school. If there was any ice in the creek, you'd have to find a free-running riffle to cross.

Most every day I would catch one or two muskrats. I would race back up over the hill, pitch them into a bucket and hang it up in the tree at the corner of the house. This was important. I did not want the hounds to get at them during the day. I would skin and stretch them after school.

Then, I would rush in and wash up some and change clothes. Mom would be setting out my breakfast. I would eat three or four sausage biscuits with thick milk gravy. Sometimes there would be fried apples, and always two or three large glasses of sweet milk and a few eggs. That would hold me until lunch. Poor Old Mrs. Stimpson was one of the cooks at Blacksburg High School. At lunchtime, I always went through her food line, since she knew that I had been along the creek in front of her house that morning, and I needed a little more food than town boys. You see, a town boy could live, quite well, on corn flakes, but I needed meat, beans, potatoes and greens. She always helped me out.

Squirrel Hunting While at School

Here is a true story about how times have changed. In the past, when I've told this story, people have looked at me like they, for sure, know it's a big one. It isn't.

The story takes place at Blacksburg High School, in the fall of the 1968 squirrel-hunting season. Lots of red-neck country boys kept a shotgun or a 22 rifle in their school lockers; not just me.

You just never knew when the leaves were going to have the correct amount of moisture in them to allow you to walk quietly through the woods. Sometimes setting in a classroom you could be looking out a window and notice that wind speed had dropped or a change in direction had occurred. Heck, a storm might suddenly be on the horizon. All boys in and around Long Shop and River Ridge knew that good squirrel hunting was coming.

Squirrel hunting was a lot like launching a rocket from Cape Canaveral. There was a very narrow window for optimal hunting, and there was no time for setting in school. So, when the time came, I very quietly left class and made my way down the hall to my locker. Fortunately, that locker was all the way at the end of the hall, which meant I was all but out the door when I got there. I gently opened my locker, filled my pockets with 12-gauge shotgun shells, picked up my trusty Plastic Stocked 12-Gauge Springfield and started to take those last few steps out the door.

Out of nowhere, there stood Mr. Bill Brown, the football coach and geography teacher. He hollered to me, "Now, just where you are going? Put that gun back in your locker and get your butt back to class."

Well, there you have it. I was back to looking out the window just like everybody else. Not one more word was said about the shotgun or trying to skip school. Today, school administration would have jacked up the school and put me under it just for having a shotgun on campus.

One day, when school was letting out, I took my old 12-gauge apart, wrapped it up in my gym clothes and got on the bus. When I asked the driver to let me off at an unscheduled stop, he looked at me hard and barked, "You are going to get in real trouble going into posted woods to squirrel hunt."

I got off the bus. I got a few squirrels, and Daddy picked me up a few hours later. No one was the wiser.

Times have changed. Some of us kept guns in our lockers. More kept guns on the racks in their pickup trucks. There was never a mean thought in any of our heads. We were just squirrel-hunters working real hard for the next day's bragging rights on the school bus, that was all.

When I was in grade school, every morning during squirrel season, I got up about 4:00 a.m. and walked out on the ridge behind the house, where there were groves of white oak and hickory. Squirrels love both of these nuts. Some mornings you could see the squirrels from the toilet when you were involved in more pressing matters. There were some mornings I shot none. Other times I would kill one; others I got two or three. I just never could get more. Yes, I was a real bad shot. Still, whatever the number, I would rush home and clean my day's catch. And, of course, I always saved the tails to show off on the school bus.

Now on the bus, there was an art to how you showed off your squirrel tails. No one, not even me, wanted to be caught with just a few tails. A high number of tails was concrete proof that you were a genuine specimen of an Appalachian Man. It kind of like measured the wildness in you. If the numbers of tails remained high over a long period of time, you might even be entitled to all the rights and privileges of a seasoned hunter. Low numbers must have indicated that you were destined to be a town person or something.

One morning I had four tails, the most I had ever killed

at once. Slowly, everyone started to show their tails. All of a sudden, I was the top hunter for the day. Now, my chest was swelling up a lot. Then Old "Big Hands" Grogan slowly showed one, then two, three. . .and four. Well, I was tied. But no, out came number five. . . six. Number seven just fell onto the bus floor. On my best day I had failed to measure up as a great squirrel hunter. I was scared to death that I was truly destined to live in town.

Seems there was a lot of truth in the little boyhood rituals. Where do I live now? Right in the middle of town with houses around me.

Sprayed By A Dead Skunk

One very cold night walking along the creek bank, not far from Mr. John Amos' honeybee hives, Terry and I happened on a real treasure, something that was going to make us some money. We found a full-grown, solid black skunk. Black hides were worth more than black and white ones. This one was frozen as hard as a rock. Maybe it was even harder than a rock. Terry said that a good prime, solid-black skunk hide was worth more than $2.00. No problem, I thought. We will melt him out some. We took the fishing ax and went to work chopping wood, and before you knew it we had a fire going. Not a regular fire, but a fire that could be seen all the way to Tom Long's Store, if anyone had been looking. We just set that frozen $2.00 skunk up on a log to thaw out, and we went on fishing.

Sometimes, I think back: What was going through Ruth and Elmer's minds to turn me loose on the creek bank to kill suckers in the middle of the winter? It was crazy to wade in the frozen creek to retrieve the fish, trap muskrats and skin old frozen skunks. One bad step, and one could fall into a frozen creek. Things like that could do more than give you a cold. I do not know what they were thinking, but I damn sure was having the time of my life until I picked up that frozen skunk.

I have put off telling you about the skunk as long as I could. I guess it is time to get it done. Please keep in mind that the skunk is worth about $2.00, we think. Most likely it would have been worth about a dime.

When we get back down to the fire from ice fishing, it has burned down low, so we add on some more wood so we can see the newly found treasure. After feeling him or her all over, we determine that the thing is still somewhat frozen. But it is skinnable.

I pull out my Queen Pocket Knife that Daddy gave me for Christmas. I am sure that it was intended for a night just like this one. The night is as cold as the steel. This is one sharp knife. It has a fine edge worked on Daddy's oil stone, plus it has been worked on the razor strop in Mason Williams' Barber Shop. At the time I had a bad habit of over-sharpening knives. You could touch the blade to your skin at the elbow and cut every hair off all the way to your wrist in one smooth motion. Sometime later I will talk about that.

Now just picture it. It is a cold night. The temperature is somewhere between 10° and 20° Fahrenheit. The creek is frozen as hard as any of the big yellow flint rocks on Shorty's hill. The air is almost still, and there is not one sound other than the crackle of that big fire and the gurgle of the open riffle not far from where I stand. The sky is clear, and all the stars are out bright and shiny as if they are watching me. As you look down the creek, there is a light gray trail of smoke, not more than 50 feet off of the ground, reaching all the way to Long Shop. There is a little crust on the snow that reflects everything.

I reach down and pick up that half-frozen $2.00 skunk with one hand. I have my razor sharp Queen Steel knife in the other. I gently pull the legs apart, and before I can start the skinning job, this dead skunk sprays me. I drop to my knees and start spitting and coughing like a skunk-sprayed coon dog. My eyes feel like they are on fire. If I had not had my eyeglasses on, the dead skunk would have blinded me. Now, I have been sprayed before, but never by a dead skunk and never at point blank range. I take to running for home, and I mean fast. All of a sudden I am very cold, I am hungry, and I genuinely smell bad. I'm thinking, "Well, if this spray is going to kill me, I wish to hell it would get on with it. I am right down miserable." But, the spray is just trying to stretch out my dying; it is playing with me like a cat plays with a mouse before it kills the thing.

When I get home everyone is asleep. I have started getting used to the smell. I still know that I smell bad, but I do not know how bad. When Mom and Daddy jump out of the bed and scream a stream of obscenities at me, I know that I am still right raw-smelling.

I am told to go back outside. They do not care that it is extremely cold. I am instructed to strip and stay there while a bath is prepared. I hit the water, and Daddy comes into the room with a great big block of lye soap and a big butcher knife. He slowly shaves the whole block into the water. "Don't even think about coming out of that water until you are blue," he growls.

As I tell Daddy the main parts of the story, he kind of chuckles under his breath. Mom just frowns, "One of these days you are going to catch rabies or something really bad, you just mark my words. Then you will be more careful about what you pick up."

The next morning I am truly better. Better is a relative term here; better than what? I do not think that I smell as bad as I did when I cleaned the hog pen. Possibly, I only smell as bad as someone who has cleaned the chicken house. Well, when I get on the bus people jump. If Cowboy White had not been on the County payroll as a bus driver, I think he would get off and let me drive.

I did get a seat that morning. In a few days it was all over. I was back to just ice fishing. But the stories about the skunk just kept growing and being told. That story kind of took on a life of its own. Some of the stuff others told I had no part in, but I just kept my mouth shut. They were right interesting, and I was willing to take the credit.

Sucker Gigging

Now, for those of you who are thinking about gigging, there was Gigging in the New River and sucker gigging in the creeks. I can bet that you have completely overlooked gigging for suckers in your remembering. Well, the fish in question is a Red Horse Sucker. They were not your regular old hogsuckers. They aren't a white sucker, neither. When I finish telling this, I might just look it up. I am going to call them suckers "Red Horses," because I just like the name best and that is what I grew up calling them.

Gigging for Red Horses isn't something new. I first learned about this from Uncle Shorty. I think that Shorty and Daddy were Red Horse Sucker Giggers from way back, but Shorty was a master. In the early spring, about the time the river water warmed up a little and the days got a little longer, the creek started to warm, too. You would hear people talking about the suckers running.

I do not know where the Red Horse Suckers live out most of their lives. I think that they live far downstream. They are a migratory fish I'm pretty sure. Once upon a time they possibly lived below the Blue Stone Dam on toward the Mississippi Valley. I don't know. I think that they are a Southern Fish! But, I do know that every spring, a few weeks before the start of trout season, the suckers would swim upstream to the smaller tributaries. They ran to places like Tom's Creek and Strouble's Creek in Merrimack. At the time of this story, I was no more than about probably 7 or 8 years old.

About every other evening, Shorty and I would go over to the double culvert down the Coal Hollow Road. Out behind a house there was a set of two culverts. They were about 15 feet high, with Norfolk and Western Railroad tracks running overhead. Water normally flowed through one, and I have no clue what the other one was for, possibly just for looks or to give me something to talk about. Anyway, you could walk right out into one culvert with the creek right at your feet. On the downstream end where there was a deep pool, the fish would stop and rest and catch their breath for little while. On the upstream end, the water was wide and shallow and no more than a foot deep. But in the middle of the culvert the water was about five feet wide and about one foot or less deep. You could almost walk up beside the Red Horses as they swam through the culvert. "Just like fishing in a kraut barrel," Uncle Shorty would say.

He also said that in his youth, just after the railroad

built these culverts, you could take three people sucker gigging. One person stood at each end and one in the middle. You did not need a gig, either; you could just snare them with a sharp forked stick. As the fish swam through the culvert, you just slipped this stick into their gills and flipped the fish up on the bank. Shorty said that you could easily catch a bucketful in a short while, and this was much better than wading in the creek and getting your feet wet.

I just never saw the number of suckers that my daddy and his brothers talked about. By the time Shorty and me were sucker-gigging, the population was way down. I think building the Blue Stone Dam stopped the migration of Red Horse Suckers. Possibly river pollution had something to do with it, too. Also could be all the people living along the creeks in the 1960s and 70s just ate a whole lot of them.

Later, I was forced to wade in the creek like a common old sucker-gigger! One of the funny stories about suckers came from Terry Albert's Long Shop Service Center. I was setting around the shop one day when I heard someone say the suckers were running, and some were going up the little branch just about the car bridge. Kittle Head Price and I ran over to see. Before you knew it Kittle Head had caught two or three with his bare hands and pitched them up on the bank. I only got one; Kittle Head was just faster than me. Three fish are not many. Again, the point of the story is by the late 1970s there were not many Red Horses, and you had to be there to get any! Also, they were small ones.

When I was about 23 years old, Walker Reid — as true a country gentleman as you'll ever meet — and I were working on the Virginia Tech Farm. A few weeks earlier, Walker had hurt his knee, and he was scheduled for surgery the very next day. We found ourselves on the bank near the mouth of the creek on Tommy Adams' Farm. The water was as cold as ice. I was out in the creek gigging the fish and pitching them to Walker for him to put in a sack. You see, since Walker was going in the next day for knee surgery, he didn't need to catch a cold.

I could not have gigged more than two or three, when I reached over to pitch one to him, and there he was, right in the creek with me. We worked the creek all the way from Whitethorn to the back of Chuck's house in Long Shop. It was late at night when we knocked on the door to try to draw him out to go fishing with us. Actually, it was very late by now, pretty damn cold, and we had not killed many fish. To my way of thinking, that was no reason not to come sucker- gigging. But since my shoes had literally dissolved on the trip up, I was standing there barefooted. Chuck did let me borrow his good dress shoes to gig back in. They were a help. The rocks were having a field day with my feet. But in the grand scheme of things, what is more important, sucker-gigging or one's feet? Is there really any need to ask such a fool question?

Another time, Perry Milton and I had driven to the mouth of the creek at Whitethorn to go sucker-gigging. Perry carried both of us in his pickup. When we got out of the truck and walked across Tommy's concrete cattle guard to get to the creek, we heard the whine of a fast car coming out of nowhere. A set of car lights just appeared. One of the locals had done turned us in to the law! Yes, sucker-gigging is illegal, too. We headed for the water rack to hide. Perry went across the water rack like a gray squirrel. I started across behind him, but I moved a little more slowly, more on the order of a three-legged groundhog. I saw the car slowing down. I just gave my gig a throw and made myself comfortable. Well, by the time the car stopped, Perry was well-hidden in the honeysuckles and kudzu on the other side. Me, on the other hand, I was setting right on top of the water rack in plain view.

When the guy asked me what I was doing, my heart sank right to the bottom. It was a voice I knew well. It was Mr. Will Hence, the county game warden. I said, "I am looking for Red Horse Suckers going by."

"Are you seeing any?" the Game Warden asked.

"No sir, my Uncle Shorty said that there were very few left, and if I ever wanted to see them, I need to look now. So here I am."

"Well, he's right about that; there sure ain't many left." He insisted on giving me a ride back to River Ridge in his car. He knew what I was up to, but he just did not see a gig. The whole time we were talking, right across the creek there was a real big dog just growling and barking its head off at us.

A little while later Perry came back to Mom's house, and

we talked about our adventure and how unlucky we were. Perry also gave me my gig. I asked him how in the world he had found it. He said that it stuck in the ground about an arm's length from him. Lucky for him I am a poor gig-thrower. It did skeer him for a few seconds, but he was a whole lot more concerned about being dog-bit. The big dog was so close Perry could smell his breath. Perry said, "Smelled like he had just eaten a cow pile or right big rotten groundhog; I thought I was next. Each time the big dog shook his head, the slobbers got on my face."

I think that was my last sucker-gigging. I do think about them suckers being all but gone now. Even today, there are very few Red Horses making the run upriver into the small creeks.

The Big Turtle

Terry Albert and I were gigging one night down near the lower island, the one near the knob. There was a great riffle just below this small island, and the water was shallow enough that you could walk across the river during the day and fish. But this night I worked the boat just below the riffle. You see, fish like the water just where the fast water meets the still water. This was where all of my uncles and others had told me that the old-timers would walk across the river at night following lamps on the banks.

This stuff was done long before the Radford Arsenal was made. If you made one wrong step, you would get wet. I always wondered why they didn't just pole the boat. We need more information on this. Who put up the lamps and kept them burning? I never saw any signs of an oil lamp. No one could ever answer this, but they kept right on telling it. Me, I'm telling it too, I guess. They even told of an old fort or something on the knob. When I went to Chuck Shorter to get more information on this subject, I learned that the word they were using was wrong. They meant to say a river *ford* was there at the knob, so my searching through the weeds, sticks, ticks and rosebushes for the old fort was a waste of time. Words do have different meaning, don't they!

We headed first this way and then back across the river. I do not think that we had even seen one good fish all night long. We were working our way back toward the old Post Office when Terry said, "Look at that big turtle." About all I could say was, "Terry, don't gig that thing." Well, I had no more than said it, when he did it and pulled it into the boat. It weighed more than 40 pounds, and he had to stand on its back to pull the gig out of its head. The monster just hissed and made funny sounds out of the big hole in his neck. I do think it was real mad, real mad for sure. Now I had not been the one that gigged it, but I am the one it took out after. That thing took one look at me and came running. It ran right slowly, but here it came, and since a boat ain't real big there was no place to hide.

I have heard stories all of my life that if one of these monsters bites you, they will not turn loose until it thunders. I guess we Appalachian Boys are just a little superstitious. I am not, but I was not going to take any chances! I was not waiting around to find out. I put the end of the boat pole right at the base of the middle seat and pole vaulted over the old turtle all the way to the front of the boat. I hit with a thud.

Terry said, "Now what are we going to do?"

When I landed I had knocked a board or two loose from the bottom. We were going down like the Titanic. Somehow we got to the bank and turned the boat over and pecked the nails back in with a river rock. We were leaking like a sieve, but we made it to the Whitethorn Boat Landing. How that monster got out, I do not know, but I am glad he did. A few days later this was right funny, but at the moment it was touch and go. I did not know whether I was going to be eaten or drown.

The Fine Art of Trotline Fishing

There is true art to laying a trotline; it is a lot easier to tell some about it than to do it. Everyone up and down the river laid trotlines; catfish were part of everybody's diet. Now what is a trotline, you be thinking? First off, the word I am explaining is *trot*, not trout. A trotline is a long fishing cord stretched across the river with many fishhooks. The main part is the running cord, and it may be as much as 100 feet or as short at 30 feet. You tie on short fishing lines about 12 to 18 inches long that are called the "bobbins." A block of wood or float is tied in the center of the running cord to mark the trotline's location and keep most of the hooks up off the bottom of the river. If you do not have a float, you had better have a very good memory and an awfully long pole to do the snagging. Big rocks or weights are tied onto the ends of the running cord so the trotline will sink and stay where you put it. Some of my lines had more than 20 hooks; most had fewer. Shorty said that in his youth they always used more.

151

For us, trotlining was a family affair. Mom would make the bobbins and often tie them on the running cord. Others took to the creek, woods, and field to catch bait. I am not going to say we needed the fish for food, but we sure did eat a lot of fish from the river. It is hard to beat catfish rolled in cornmeal, fried eggs and fried green tomatoes and sweet milk for breakfast. If you are going to find something better, you are going to work at it.

Now, if you tangled your line, you just as well have headed home. All it took was getting your foot caught in the line one time to create one giant knot. You were never going to get it straightened out ever again, ever. So, laying trotlines required sober, steady, patient hands and coordinated feet. That left all of the Lytton clan out. All of them added together did not possess one of the four required virtues. So when the family laid trotlines, you had to get ready for lot of bad tempers, hollering, cussing, and finger-pointing.

At my peak of trotlining. we would set 20 or more on a weekend. We used catalpa worms for bait. By now I was smarter and lazier. Catalpa caterpillars are very ugly with that big stinger and all, but the catfish do love them. A great stinger,but they can't sting; if they could have, it would leave a pump knot as big as a walnut. We were not too lazy to catch bait the way Daddy, Shorty and Nelson had; the bait just wasn't to be had. You would have had to walk way back behind the dump in Wake Forest to the old stone quarry just to catch up a few black lizards. Twenty or thirty years earlier big black lizards could be found all over the county in all the cool shady spring branches.

The poor New River was changing just as I was. I think the river knew of this change, for she had seen change all of her flowing days. I had not; I was just discovering the river and it all looked fresh and new to me and just full of new adventures. I do think that the Old River took me by the hand and guided me. I guess that is why they made history books, just so I could remember these times and things. Maybe, just maybe, I ought to go to the Whiterock and sit for a few hours and look again. Just to remember.

To me this story about boat-riding and trotline-fishing always sounds like a picture on a calendar from the feed store looks. Why in the world did I wait so long to get myself born? In my youth, while I was paddling the boat upriver, I would pass the place where we grew corn for the hogs and roasting ears for gigging, past the place where my old cinder block cabin would someday stand. Both Daddy and Shorty said, "Things change and sometimes they change fast. Some of the things take their time. Someday you will see what I mean." I guess someday is today.

Like my father and uncles, I, too, became a good trotliner. Back in 1968, when the catalpa trees were covered with catalpa caterpillars, we took to laying trotlines. We would lay the first one almost in front of the bus and one just below each ledge upriver, until we either ran out of bait, or ran out of trotlines, or for sure when we ran out of beer. Either of the three would send you to the bank real quick like.

The main operations center for this activity was commonly referred to as "the bus." That is where everything was kept. Once all the trotlines were in the water, about every hour someone would take the boat out for a turn, checking the lines. It was simple. You picked up the float, grabbed the running cord and moved left then right. You put on new bait, took off a fish or two and removed all trash or river weeds that may have collected on the trotline.

We never caught that many fish compared to the hours we put in, but that was never the point. We were true-blue, honest-to-goodness trotliners. We were part of the old tradition, and the real stories live on through us. We were doing the things that grown men on River Ridge did. Sometimes these real men would even join in the ritual with us boys. Like the times Uncle Fred would drive up from Richmond just to set in the boat when we checked the trotlines. He would smile, laugh and tell the same old stories. As I look back I realize so very much time was put into laying the lines in the exact spots where the history of catching fish was. I may not have caught the fish, but I did understand the history of it all.

The Best Fish I Ever Saw

I love to fish; I always have. I will bet you that no one ever fished the New River more than me. I have fished when the big pieces of ice made it hard to keep a line on the bottom. I have fished with trotlines. I have poled gigging boats from Fishin Run up past Lover's Leap all the way to the arsenal. I have waded every ledge that I could. I have swum over the others. I have used every kind of bait there is, and I have never managed to catch one big fish in my whole life.

But, I was a good guide. It seemed like everyone that fished with me caught good fish. For example, my cousin Bruce and I went fishing when he was about 10 years old. We crossed the river in front of the bus and waded out on the first ledge. Bruce caught a 2 ½- or 3-pound bass; this was bigger than any I ever caught.

I think it was late February 1971 when Hoc Wilson and I were working the north bank just above Whitethorn. You guessed it. The bass was bigger than any fish I ever caught. Hoc didn't even know he had caught it, thought that his line was hung.

Ronald Billups and I fished together a lot, and he always caught more big fish than anyone I ever met. I might catch as many pounds of fish, but not the big ones. Ronald and I were talking one day to a friend of his. Ronald said, "Go fishing with Charles; he will show you where the big ones are." We did and I did. He caught a small-mouth weighing 4 ½ pounds right in front of Mod Snider's cabin. It happened so fast that I did not even have time to put any bait on my line. I must have fished there a thousand times. I just went to the bank and on to the cabin.

Now I did catch a big muskie one time. I was working a six-inch green minnow lure along a ledge coming out of the Whiterock Hole. It was the first time I had ever used the plug, and it was the biggest plug I had ever seen. It was running about 15 feet deep, when all of sudden something took it and started downriver hard. I got the fish in the boat, and I am guessing it would have weighed 15 or more pounds. You see, I unhooked the muskie and promptly dropped it back in the river. Yes, I went home swearing I would never fish again! The men cat-fishing at the Whiterock just laughed and told me that my bad fishing record was still good. They told that story for weeks!

There is a deep hole just under the riffle at Lover's Leap. This is where the most exciting catch I ever was a party to happened. To start with, I did not catch the big fish, but I do claim credit for setting the greatest fish hunt in my time in motion. I also passed the mantle on to younger trotliners, in true Huckleberry Finn fashion.

I had caught a big Channel Cat that might have weighed 8 or 9 pounds. In my time, this was a big catfish. While he was on the line, his side had been scraped to the bone by a bigger fish; his tail was just about digested. That rascal just tried to swallow him and must have weighed 50 pounds or more. I know that I fished for this elusive giant for weeks. I never saw the fish or even got another bite. When I lost interest, Rocky and Robin Henry took up where I left off. Within a few weeks they caught him. Now, they were young boys, probably no more than 8 or 9 years old at the time. Today, I think that they did a good job. In some ways they were a lot like me. When I saw the big fish, I kind of felt sorry for him. He weighed more than 50 pounds, but he was still thin and poor-looking. When they butchered him, they discovered a large rock in his gut. That might have affected his eating habits. But he was old, far older than me!

The boys said that they had hooked an even larger one, but lost him trying to bring him up to the boat. The fish was so large that the boys were afraid to stick their hands in the mouth to hold onto him. Before they could muster up enough nerve, the big fish broke the line and slowly swam off. Fifty years later this story is still being told by men somewhat younger than me. Man oh man, the New River is something.

The second biggest catfish I ever saw Jimmy Bland gigged. Buck Rider wanted a ride upriver one night really late. There was a lady that he sometimes visited when the night air was just right and the stars shown bright. The night air was just right, so Jimmy and I took him about as far upriver as we could go and let him out. Mr. Buck then struck out overland on foot.

We were to come back for him in a few hours, so we went gigging in and around the shallow rock bars near the Radford Arsenal. Truly it was a poor night for gigging fish. The wind was up a little, and the water had a slight dingy color about it. We had a third person in the boat with us: Old Preacher Wiggins. No, he was not a preacher, he just liked fish gigging and kind of liked the nickname. He was sitting on the middle seat this night. Every once in a while, lightning would flash. Jimmy would take to cussing, and Preacher would say, "Now boy don't be cussin' no lightning." Each flash, the two would say the same thing over and over.

We had not killed more than 10 or 15 pounds of fish, when Mr. Buck whistled. We started across the river following a deep ledge. Just as the shallow rock bar came good and clear, there was one of the biggest mud cats I had ever seen. Jimmy got him. We bragged about him all the way to the cabin. As we pulled in, there stood Mrs. Rider, who asked where we had been. Mr. Buck Rider answered back, "Why, honeybunch, we have been gigging, and look here at this big catfish I gigged. Now, Jimmy, I know that you have never eaten any big catfish filets, so you just keep him." So we caught him, but we did not really get to brag on him.

Daddy, Buck and I were gigging one night, and Daddy whispered to Buck to hold the boat real still and move forward a few feet. Daddy then gigged the biggest pike they had ever seen; must have weighed more than 25 pounds. It had big teeth, too. Well, they looked him over and determined that he was some new kind of new pike. No one knew he was muskie, and I bet if "The Man" had caught us with that muskie, he'd have put us in jail and thrown away the key. We left in a hurry with the prize. In just a short time, the big muskie was cleaned by truck lights and divided up.

Stanley Russell, who was married to my cousin, Millie, and I had about the same luck fishing. He, too, wanted to catch one big fish that he could have mounted on the wall. One night, he and I were sitting in the middle, while Mod Snider moved the boat across the river between the two islands just below the barrel, where there was a very small gravel pile, a fish nest. Elmer asked Mod to move closer to the nest. About this time, a very large small-mouth bass swam right in front of the boat. Stanley pleaded with Daddy not to gig it, but Daddy did anyway. Stanley just held the fish all the way back to the bank. "I have fished for that one all of my life, and now you have killed him," he said. I thought that Stanley might cry. Quietly, I hoped he would. This bunch of men had no feeling for the living or the dead or anything, and I wanted to watch Stanley cry. But he did not.

Another time, Marvin Weeks and I were working the boat in this same region of the river. Marvin gigged a redeye that weighed far more than a pound. He did not have a hole in him, but he did have two very bad scrapes on his sides. We wanted to enter him in a fishing contest Press Brown Sporting Goods Store was having, but we could not figure a way to cover up the big scratches. That fish stayed in the freezer at home for two or three years. I showed it to everyone that would look. One day, I just fed him to all the cats living around the back building. What a waste of a fine fish!

Chuck Shorter gigged one of the biggest coon-tail perches ever to come out of the river. Like with the big bass and redeye, about all you can do is eat it and wait 50 years before you tell someone. This was the night we were all testing out our moonshine-drinking skills, and Chuck fell out of the boat -- well almost. He got his legs hung under the middle seat, and he almost drowned before we got his legs a-loose so he could topple on over into the river. He made it, and we went on gigging and working on the shine.

Muskrat Trapping on the New River

I know that I have already talked about muskrat trapping, but that was on Tom's Creek. Trapping on the New River was a much different experience, so different techniques were required. On the creek there were very few people; on the river there were lots.

On the New River you could set traps almost everywhere. The population of muskrats was also very high, and they were truly destroying the riverbank. Prime hides were bringing $1.50 apiece. Opportunity was limitless, but not without peril. I used my old canoe to set traps on both sides of the river. I trapped from the cabin all the way to Lovers Leap, and to the edge of the Radford Arsenal Property. Sometimes I set as many as 40 traps. A lot of people only set traps on the railroad side so they could check their traps on foot. They were just too afraid of the river in the winter. It was a great place to get yourself froze to death before you had the time to drown. Sometimes I wish I had been a little more cautious, but I wasn't. I do think that I am very lucky to be writing this.

I always had to check traps after work. It was way after dark when I finished. Trapping is like dairy farming— you got to milk them cows every day. I checked traps when it was clear, raining or snowing. They had to be checked every night, no matter what.

I always liked the snow. It made the river the prettiest place on this earth. When I was younger, the river came up about 9:00 a.m. when the power company was generating electricity at the hydroelectric plant in Radford. The water lowered by 3:00 p.m. each evening. That meant when nighttime came, the river was low and the riverbank had dried off real nice. On snowy nights with a full moon, it became a true winter wonderland. Few have ever ventured out to see or experience such freedom and beauty.

Fresh snow formed a cap on each rock in the middle of the river by the old barrel. There was a very clean, clear black line at the water's edge. Sometimes you could see muskrats setting on the snow-covered rocks eating freshwater mussels and big crawfish that they had picked up from the river. The moon and stars were bright enough that I could paddle the river and check the traps without a light. Bare-limbed trees cast nighttime shadows halfway across the river. There was never a thought given to the danger or the cold water temperature or hypothermia. Heck, I did not even know what that was.

This here is the hard part of this story to tell. It was truly magnificent, and I would like for you to picture it, too. Close your eyes for a moment. OK, OK, have someone read it to you. Well, anyway, all of this took place long before Al Gore invented Global Warming. It was 1972 or thereabout. For a few days the mercury had stayed below 0 degrees Fahrenheit, and it had been a few weeks since the thermometer had gotten much above freezing.

At that time, I was working at the Moore Farm that belongs to Virginia Tech. We were spending as much time digging up frozen water lines and fixing water leaks as we were feeding cattle and sheep. The soil was frozen solid down more than 15 inches deep. This all made muskrat-trapping much harder, a lot more fun and extremely dangerous! But, heck, I was 20 years old and full of that good old Appalachian Man Syndrome. Another way to say that is I just did not care one little bit.

The river was spectacular on those starry cold nights. One night in particular, Bogan Albright had come to the cabin to help check muskrat traps. I think that this was only fair, since we were partners in this trapping venture. Now, to be honest here, it might not sound real manly, but the night itself just might have brought him out. You see it was very cold, for sure. No one but a truest red-neck boy or a crazy man would be about to do what we were thinking. First, we built up a right big fire in the cabin's fireplace and banked it off with a big pile of almost green wood so there would be a fire when we got back.

We took the canoe out of the cabin and locked the door so Jim Dog could not push it open. It was so cold that I had to keep the canoe in the cabin. It was much easier to get it out the door than to pull and jerk on it to break it free from the frozen ground outside. Here is a question that I have asked myself more than once: Why in the mortal heck were we not using the flat-bottom boat? It was more stable, had a lot more room, was much safer, and it could be chopped out of the ice in the time it took to drag the canoe out of the cabin. I will just keep thinking on this question.

We got the canoe into the water, and I started it upriver. There were very narrow ice channels in the river, some no more than three or four feet wide. The ice was no more than ½" to ¾" thick. It would all be broken up in a few hours when the folks at the Radford Dam started generating electricity again, but right then it was there and as real as it gets.

When we got near the traps, Bogan had to lean over the front of the canoe, use the paddle to chop a channel through the ice to the trap, run his naked arm down into the water to reach it, and then pick it up to see if we had caught a muskrat. If yes, he put the animal in the canoe and reset the trap. (This is a lot easier, a hell of a lot easier, when you had a second person in the canoe. Often I did this by myself.) If we had not caught anything, he still had to reset the trap. It was cold, real cold work.

After about ten or so traps, Bogan was starting to get cold. We always took us a break when he was cold. We just stopped paddling and let the canoe drift wherever it wanted to go, while we settled down to drinking ourselves a little Kentucky Gentleman. Both of us brought our own bottle. We did this for health reasons; one of us was generally sick with a cold from playing in a frozen river. We did not want to pass around bad germs and the like. No chaser was needed; you kind of liked the warm burn. Now, keep in mind that the air temperature was most likely around 10 or 15 degrees at best.

As we sipped our Kentucky Gentleman right out of the bottle and lit up a Winston cigarette or my trusty pipe and just kind of rared back on that cold metal seat, there was not one trace of air stirring. There was a small column of steam or fog coming off of Bogan. It went up about 10 or so feet and just kind of vanished into the night. I know this because the steam just set there for a long while, going nowhere. I can bet there was one coming off my body, too. Sounds from ice cracking on the riverbank reached all the way across the river. As you exhaled the smoke, it didn't go anywhere either. Instead, the smoke kind of stayed near the canoe and a few inches above the ice and very slowly thinned and then vanished in the moonlight and starlight.

I am sure that God has made a lot of great places. He just had to, for it is one big Earth. But, I do not think that he has ever spent as much time on one place as he did on the New River in the winter of 1972. God knows all and when He was making this place, I bet He had me in mind. That day when He drew up the plan for the New River and dreamed up winter and muskrat trapping, it was all just for a night like this one.

On one night in particular—I don't think it was this same one —the snow was falling ever so lightly, and the flakes were big. The river was so still and quiet you could hear the snow as it fell to the ice. Every snowflake may be different, but their sound is about the same. I have trouble describing this sound: it was like listening to one single solitary leaf falling from a big red oak to the ground while squirrel hunting. You know it was real quiet, but the sound was still there.

When you're trapping, though, even after the big drink of Kentucky Gentleman, you realize that your hands are frozen and you had better get on with the task at hand.

God willing, tomorrow night will come too. And again I will be right here. But right now I need to stand in front of the cabin fire.

I never once gave much thought to the canoe flipping over. Old Jim Dog did try his best to flip the canoe a time or two, but he failed. I also never gave one thought to falling out of the canoe. I never thought about anything except what a great time this was to be young and crazy enough to check muskrat traps by moonlight on a frozen river. Young Appalachian Men from River Ridge once liked things like that! Well, you can't do that today. Heck, Old Al Gore took care of that when he got caught up in a whirl with that global warming thing.

I think that this was the winter that Mary Elizabeth got sick for the first time too. Mary Elizabeth was Bogan's little girl. She was about three at the time, and in less than three years she had died of leukemia. I got married and life was just different somehow. I rarely went to the river much anymore and never in the winter. Oh heck, what can I say? That sweet smell of wood smoke and perfume does have a profound effect on a man's thinking.

The Sweet Smell of Wood Smoke and Perfume

Like I have stated more than once, I lived along the New River. I swam in it, I caught fish from it, and I ate vegetables grown in large gardens planted on its banks. I smelled the wildflowers that grew along the river and railroad right-of-way. On occasion, I even drank its questionable water, but never once did it make me sick. I think it only made me stronger. The old river liked me back; somehow I knew this. I camped along the bank and called an old school bus my house. My life existed in a four-or-five-mile span of New River, between the riffle at Fish Run to just above Lover's Leap. Up until now I had about everything I had ever wanted! I can even remember some of my friends saying that they wished they could live the way I did.

Little did I know that my life was fixing to change. Why, my world was going to expand a million-fold. The old river had yet another experience in store for me. I must admit that at this point, my knowledge of the fairer sex was right limited. I had been around a few ladies, but none could hold my interest very long the way the river could. They just did not like fried potatoes and fried fish every meal and boys with the smell of the riverbanks ground into their skin. For me, there was something about an endless blue sky twinkling on the clear water or the smell of fresh-caught fish frying over an open fire or the taste of the air after a sweet summer rain or the snow piled up on rocks out in the river. The shine of the slick mud was good, too.

One fine day, two of my closest friends came to the bus for a swim and a little small-mouth bass fishing. I thought that wading the riffles below the Little Island would be the best place to accomplish both missions. You know, seine up a few hellgrammites or crawfish and walk the shallow riffle.

So, down the river we go. After a few hours of fishing and swimming, we walk up onto the Big Island, where I had one of my many little camps. We set down on big logs and light up one of them Marlboro cigarettes and drink a Blue Ribbon beer cooled in the river. The sun is making gray slow-moving patterns on the ground, the way it does when it has its way with the tree canopy.

Why, the Marlboro Man himself and all of his horseback-riding in the tv commercials did not represent a more complete picture of tranquility and young manhood. (I met the Marlboro Man in San Francisco one time. He wasn't as tall as you might think, but his cigarettes were sure good and comforting.) This, right here, was what life was supposed to be like.

After a few minutes my friends announce that they need to head back to town and clean up; they both have dates. At about the same time, they both say, "Why don't we bring the girls down here tonight for a late evening boat ride and picnic? Will you pole us around on the moonlit river in the barge? Will you bring all of us down to this spot for a picnic? We will bring hotdogs and cold beer."

If the truth be known, I was a hell of riverboat poler and river man, none better had I seen before or since, and I have known some of the best. Why, I could push that old barge about anywhere anyone would ever want to go. But, my skill as one of those Italian men that pole those gondolas was yet unknown and untested. I could not sing much and never found anyone that even wanted to hear it. When it came to being around the fairer sex, I had at least two left feet and never knew what to say, either.

Well, anyway, they depart for home and a good, hot-water bath. I start making ready for my evening guests by sweeping the old barge with a stiff broom to break loose all of the fish guts and dried mud. I then dip the old boat full of water a few times to rinse out the last of the guts, scales and mud. Once it is clean and smelling good, I put the flat "setting-on" blocks of wood and the old armchair back in the barge. With this many people, I would need extra seating. (As I think back, those blocks were very big blocks with monster knots that I could not bust for firewood; they weighed a ton.)

I just strip down buck naked on the riverbank. I then

take me a bath in the river, myself, and wash my clothes at the same time. I do not have any soap. I never before have had a need for any soap along the river. I put my clothes on willow bushes and clumps of Johnson Grass so they will be dry when my company arrives. True to my red-neck Appalachian ways, I just set buck naked on the bank fishing until my clothes dry. I am not dirt-streaked or anything, but not real clean either. When I dress I don't smell too bad, just kind of stale or something. I guess you could say I was earthy, real earthy or maybe had a riverish air about me.

True to their word, just before dark my two friends return with their girlfriends. As they unload that little car, I immediately start to feel uncomfortable. They all smell clean; they have on fresh, unworn clothes. I can just bet none of them has bathed in the river without a bar of soap or dried their week-old clothes draped across tall weeds. They have on shoes, too. I have on an old worn-out pair of Radford Arsenal shoes.

Over the next few minutes, we load the beer, food and other stuff into the old barge. Now the old barge has had a few big loads in the past, but few if any larger than this one. As soon as we push off, I know that I need to be pushing the boat upriver, not down. Downstream the water is swifter, and from there it will be a hard trip back.

I do not know if I was under the influence of cold beer or sweet-smelling perfume the most; likely it was a lot of both. Both are right highly influential things. Anyway, downstream we go. From the bus to the Big Island is no more than three quarters of a mile. In just a few minutes, I am picking my way past the barrel and the shallow rock bar, then down between the head of the two islands. The shadows of the big trees almost turn the lights off, and there is only a little bit of red color in the sky that comes down to the river. You know, I might just make a gondolier poler yet.

It is very pretty, with a clear sky, long shadows and the sweet smells coming off the river. Heat lightning makes streaks across the early evening sky. I run the barge up on a weedy rock bar and drop the tie plate anchor over a big tree root. Everyone makes their way to the fire ring. We start a fire and cook our hotdogs and hamburgers, then drink up a good cold beer. I sit by the fire, smoke my pipe and listen to the talk.

After a while, an hour or two, I decide I'll go get some more firewood and check on the river. I bring back enough wood to make a fire big enough to see all the way to Whitethorn. The fire crackles and smoke rises right straight through the trees. You can see the light, whitish green color of the underside of each and every leaf. The leaves move in the rising heat, too.

After another short while when I go to check on the barge, I find out that the river has come up a lot, so much that I have to wade out into the river to get the tie plate.

When I bring the boat ashore, I know that I am fixing to earn those hot dogs, cigarettes and free beer. All of that heat lightning weren't no heat lighting at all. It is a big thunderstorm upriver.

I go back to the fire and explain our situation. There has been a big rain upstream, and the Radford Dam people have released a lot of water into the river so that it is now running full and swift. The best thing is to set tight for five or six hours, and let the river go back down.

I am told that this is not an option. We load everything back into the barge and push off. I have a 14-foot poplar boat pole. Standing right tall on the back seat, I quickly push the pole to the bottom of the river and push the boat forward eight or ten feet. Before I can lift the pole and repeat the process, the fast water pushes the barge back downstream. I do this for five or ten minutes, and we move upstream no more than a few feet or so. One of my guests says, "We are not moving much at all. What are we going to do?"

I explain the options. One thing we can do is to go down-river to the boat landing at Whitethorn. It is on the other side of the river and downstream below the Big Island. We would then walk up the railroad track to the bus. From the looks of every-one's faces, this is not going be an option either. Another option is to go downstream and try for the Arsenal side of the river. There is less current on that side. What I want to say is, "Oh hell, I am having a heart attack back here, and I am about dead already. My arms and feet are just about to fall off." But no, the smell of sweet female perfume with the hint of wood smoke has its hold on me. I say, "We can try the Arsenal side."

No one but me has a clue as to what is going on. The river is still coming up and quickly. If we try the Arsenal side and cannot get upriver, most likely I won't be able to get the barge back across the river quick enough to make the boat landing at Whitethorne. We will end up landing down in Don Gwynn's bottom. That would mean mud, brush and lots of black willows to fight. Then we will have to either hitch a ride home or walk up the tracks to the bus. But, I do not say a word about this possibility. I just keep smelling the sweet female perfume. I do this while I sweat and lather up like an overworked plow horse in the spring and breathe like the little dinky engine used to pull coal out of the Big Vein.

Well, I stick so close to the Arsenal bank that the tree limbs are brushing the sides of the barge. It is very slow and hard going, but we are making steady progress. Every once in awhile, one of my passengers hands me a half-drank Blue Ribbon beer or a half-smoked Marlboro. I would like to have had a full one. Gulp and puff, then keep the pole pushing its way to the bottom. They just keep talking and laughing.

I guess I just keep up smelling that female perfume. I am also starting to smell that river-washed shirt a little. I decide I need to get a bar of Ivory Soap, poke a hole in it and tie it to a tree for emergencies. Right now, it might just help out a little.

I get just about to the rock bar across from the bus. I turn the barge across the river and within a second the current starts pulling me downriver. Using the pole as a paddle, I work with the speed of a paddlewheel on a riverboat. I hit solid river bottom just above Mod Snider's Cabin, and now I start up the river to the bus. In just a little while, we tie the barge to the bank. I am so tired that I can hardly move my arms, and my back is just give out. My poor old feet have no feeling. Normally, the return trip upriver would not take more than 25 to 30 minutes. Tonight it has taken close to two hours.

Two things to note here. First off, at no time was anyone in any real danger. Up around the islands, the river is wide and flat. My pride was a little shaken, but if I had had to make a break for Donald Gwynn's Bottom, the locals would still be laughing at me. I did get to come home with some pride intact. Second, I did enjoy the sweet smell of a woman's perfume. It seemed to affect me in way it never had before, and I did not mind it at all.

Miss Gail and I were fishing in this same spot not long ago. I pulled the old red canoe up on the grassy rock and sand bar, where it came to rest a foot above the water line. The canoe was never going anywhere, but because of memories of the past or old river boy instincts, I took the anchor over to the shore and dropped it over a root. It might have been the same exact root from 50 years ago. I had not thought about this little story until I heard the clink of anchor on the rocks. I had a wonderful chuckle under my breath. I waded back to Gail and told her that she was okay now to set back and read, if she wished.

You Can Learn a Lot From a Groundhog!

On River Ridge, everything presented to you has an important life lesson, and I tended to grow up right fast. I am guessing that I was about ten years old or younger. Daddy and I were walking up the railroad tracks toward the Tommy Bottom. Where we were going I do not know. We passed the Whiterock, when Pappy saw a very young groundhog. He was about as big as Daddy's fist and weighed no more than two pounds. The little varmint was digging a new hole to crawl in. Pappy and me set down on a rail, yes, right out in the hot sun, and watched the little animal dig. We watched him sling dirt for a good half an hour before Daddy spoke.

Daddy said, "Do you see him digging in the soft dirt near the base of the hill? When it rains the hole will fill with water and the groundhog might drown. He looks little for this job doesn't he?"

"I reckon" I said. I did not know exactly where he was

going with this story.

Daddy said "When a young groundhog gets so big, the mother groundhog bites him on the ear and drags him out of the den. This is done until he cannot stand the biting anymore. Soon he gets the idea that he is on his own, and he takes to running.

"When he gets real tired of running, he is full grown and on his own. He then remembers that he needs to be sleeping underground. It is much cooler and safer! Outside in the open he is going to get eaten by a fox or a hawk. So he goes to digging a new hole quickly.

"In life, you got to grow up, and I mean grow up fast. Since this little groundhog did not pay much attention to its momma when she was talking about hole-digging, most likely he will get himself drowned or eaten.

"Now, as for you, there will come a day when Ruth and I will tell you to get your butt out of the house and don't come back. You will be grown on that day. You will be on your own, so make sure you hear these little stories. Being on your own takes more time, money and experience than you think."

You might ask me what I learned from this lesson. Hell, I don't know, and that is for sure. I don't think that I slept very well for a few nights. I was just wondering if tomorrow might be the day that they were going to grab me by the ear and pitch me out. I didn't even know where town was yet. Maybe I could work on the Big Farm, but that meant Bill "Mad Dog" Graves might just ring my neck off, or something.

When morning came, I thought, "Well, it is daylight now, and I am still here so they must have decided to put up with me for one more day at least.

"Charles," I would think to myself, "eat a lot for it might be a day or two before you catch on somewhere else."

Miss Gail has said to me more than once that I was raised by wolves. Then, when she's thought a little more, she changes her mind a little. "No, I don't think so," she shakes her head. "Wolves have family units where they hunt together, work together and even set up housekeeping together."

Earlier on I thought that I would get the boot any day. But I did not. I just seemed to hang around the River Ridge all of my life. I will tell you one thing; I have never forgotten that life lesson and the little groundhog. I someday hope to know that I have made it. I wonder if the little groundhog ever did?

I have always thought that this was a real good story about life, and I wanted to tell someone. But the more I thought about it, I think Daddy was just full of leftover fried peach pies, fried eggs, hot butter biscuits, sausage cakes, apple butter, strong coffee, sausage gravy and lots of sweet milk -- all we had had for breakfast at his mother's house that morning. After we had eaten at our house, we went over the hill and mooched off a second breakfast from Grandmother. She lived about one hundred yards from my house.

Stop and think about this. Mamaw never bit his ear and ran him off did she? She might have wished she had a few times. He'd lived up on the hill above her house all of his adult life. Yeah, he was just enjoying the story. That sorry-assed rascal.

To Some, They Are Just Memories; To Me, They Make Up My Life

Last night there was a full moon, and the sky was as clear as crystal. About midnight, I walked out into my yard just to look at the night sky. When I stepped onto the grass, my mind was flooded with thousands of memories of nights just like this one. I just kind of fell into an old lawn chair. I enjoyed the sights and sounds until there was a little bit of light showing in the east.

The air was warm and clean. The grass was wet, not with rain, but cool with dew. Long, pale shadows stretched across the yard. Yes, there was just enough moonlight to see the sunflowers that had grown tall. Their shadows stretched all the way across the yard.

Down over the hill, the thick fog held close to the ground, forming a thick blanket over the little valley, before slowly inching its way up the hill toward me.

Times do change but some things just never do. Like my memories of New River, fine friends and the many of life's little twists. The Old River never stops giving.

I was riding my small boat upriver a few days ago. The water was so clear that I could see each and every ledge as I passed over. The Whiterock was tall and inviting, too. Chasing the brightly colored reflections of trees in the water, I thought about gigging catfish and setting trotlines on cool nights long ago. I even imagined me once again setting on the Whiterock, waiting for morning to come.

There are new memories, too. Recently, on a boat ride up New River, I had two small boogie boards attached to the back, and a little granddaughter on each. Their laughter was almost as loud as my little 4.5 horsepower Johnson Outboard Motor.

This was fun, and they now have a memory implanted in their minds that will last a lifetime. We rode from the bus all the way to the big riffle at Lover's Leap and back. As we passed other boats and fisherman, they quickly joined in the fun and laughter.

Yes, *The Cool Side of the Pillow* is filled with memories, and I hope you have enjoyed reading them as much as I have enjoyed both living them and writing about my life on River Ridge. Take a walk or a late night swim tonight, you just never know what or who will turn up. I can bet that you will not forget this night! You ort to take a copy of *The Cool Side of the Pillow* with you, too.

As I have read and re-read this book, I've thought a lot about the first statement made in the movie "A River Runs Through It," based on Norman MacLean's best-selling book.

The statement goes something like, "In our family, there is no clear line between religion and trout fly fishing." As for me, I don't think there is clear line between New River, River Ridge and any other place on Mother Earth. I was just born lucky!